Healing With Pleasure Medicine
Unearthing the Beautiful, Sensual and Sexual You

© 2014 Betty Louise

First Edition

All Rights Reserved. The author grants no assignable permission to reproduce for resale or redistribution. This license is limited to the individual purchaser and does not extend to others. Permission to reproduce these materials for any other purpose must be obtained in writing from the publisher except for the use of brief quotations within book chapters.

Disclaimer

This book is not intended to be a substitute for professional care, or a treatment for any mental or physical condition. Different things work for different people. Although these ideas and concepts have helped many people, everyone is different. Sometimes a story or thought might stir up uncomfortable feelings, especially if you have a traumatic history. If this is the case, seeking professional help or even discussing it with a friend may help. Change the thought in some way so it fits for you, or just move on. Be kind to yourself. Being nonjudgmental and not beating yourself up is extremely important. Often we are kinder to others than to ourselves.

My inner wisdom and the amazing support of the people I have in my life have been my guiding light, helping me through many life challenges. Many people find their spiritual connection in religion. Please note that I write from my beliefs and do not mean to impose them onto you. I believe it's important for us all to find our own path to love, wisdom and faith. It is important to believe that we are loved and deserve the life we want. Values and beliefs are individual choices.

To listen to the complete interviews and obtain free bonuses, visit www.coachbettylive.com.

Published by M&B Global Solutions Inc.
United States of America (USA)
ISBN: 978-1-942731-09-2

Healing With Pleasure Medicine

Unearthing the Beautiful, Sensual and Sexual You

By Betty Louise

What Experts Are Saying About Coach Betty Louise

and

"Healing With Pleasure Medicine"

"I love Coach Betty's approach to peace, passion and pleasure. She is a spirit of joy, and her book is a beautiful reflection of that."
    Anne-Louise Sterry, International Speaker and Performer

****

"Coach Betty brings together an illustrious lineup of experts, intriguing client stories and personal anecdotes which make 'Healing with Pleasure Medicine' one of the more reader-friendly books I have read in a long time. I am particularly inspired by the level of enthusiasm and joy she models for us despite her chronic pain. If Coach Betty can find this much joy in life, what excuse do we have?"
    Veronica Monet, ACS, CAM, host of The Shame Free Zone

****

"Betty's got her own tempo. Somehow the secret in life is to walk on the rhythm of your heartbeat. She knows that and is always pleased to dance on such a deep beat in harmony with Mother Nature."
    Fabrice Mareau (Fa Musician)

****

"I love Coach Betty's simple and fun approach to finding pleasure medicine. She also presents a compelling case to ponder a new vision of how loving life is a genuine path to healing."
    Kim Corbin, Senior Publicist, New World Library

"From my experience, women need to be empowered and run the world. The feminine is healing for us all. The healing power of pleasure will only come to women when they give up submissiveness and role playing, find their authentic selves and express their power in a healthy way. Women are the source of life and without them all life would end. So achieve your potential, keep your power and use it to bring pleasure to yourselves and all life. 'Healing With Pleasure Medicine' can be your guidebook to the life you deserve."

Bernie Siegel, MD
Author of "A Book of Miracles" and "The Art of Healing"

****

"I have worked with various life and career coaches, and I don't know of another person that can help people become more positive, focus on pleasure, and recognize their own magnificence more than Coach Betty Louise. This is a must-read if you are unable to see your own beauty and feel your sensuality. Come on ladies … time for another revolution!"

Annie Spiegelman, Author of "Talking Dirt: The Dirt Diva's Guide to Organic Gardening"

Dedication

This book is dedicated to the beautiful inner essence in ALL women!

Contents

Acknowledgements 11
Preface 13

Part 1: PAUSE 19
1. The Day That Marvin Gaye Spoke to Me 21
2. PAUSE: The Main Ingredient in the Pleasure Prescription 29
3. No Multitasking – Please 35
4. Ask for What You Want and Need 41
5. Notice What Works Well 45
6. Looking for Pleasure in All the Right Places 49
7. Case Studies of PAUSE for Pleasure 55
8. Moving to Pleasure 63
9. What's Next? 65

Part 2: PONDER 67
1. What does it really mean to PONDER 69
2. Your 100 Percent Pure Energy 75
3. Positive/Optimism/Perspectives 81
4. Sensuality and Self Love 89
5. Half Empty? Half Full? 101
6. The Story You Tell Yourself Matters 107
7. The Healing Power of Music and Sound 113
8. Future World to PONDER 121
9. Moving to Pleasure, Part II 129

Part 3: PULSE **133**
1. The Wisdom of Your Body 135
2. Self-Pleasure 141
3. Meet Point Dance 145
4. Channeling Sensual Energy into Ordinary Experiences 151
5. Ground in The Truth 157
6. How Your Energy Impacts and Influences 163

Putting It All Together for a Global Healing 169
Resources 174
About the Author 178

Acknowledgements

I would like to acknowledge some dear people who made significant contributions to my journey and writing this book. My daughter, Rebecca Davie, who always writes how much she believes in me; my sister, Vicki Dotterer, for her undying support and love; my BFF, Karen Carlson, who can make me laugh like no other; and Annie Spiegelman, who keeps loving me no matter where my journey takes me.

And finally, this would absolutely not have happened in the time frame it did without the support of my entrepreneurial coach, Bonnie Groessl. Her loving and expert guidance made the whole experience flow.

Preface

We, as human beings, have forgotten about simple pleasures that can transform our life into more fulfillment and meaning. By the time you finish reading this book, you will be more aware of your natural beauty, sensuality and sexuality. Your receptivity to pleasure will increase, and that means more easy fun and joy.

I wrote this book because I see and feel the need for more positive energy (from both men and women) in the world. We have an epidemic of chronic pain and anger that sometimes can be so far under the surface that it goes unrecognized. Whether you know you have pain and anger or not, the antidote is Pleasure Medicine. Who couldn't use a little more pleasure in their life?

I want women and mindful men to step into their true natural power, which to my mind, stems from inner beauty and inner sexuality. It's like being and living in your pure and natural magnificence, minus the ego.

I continue to learn so much about how to live a full and rich life while dealing with a very challenging health condition. The fact that I have been able to access a place of pure pleasure on a regular basis in the middle of debilitating pain all over my body is quite miraculous, even in my humble eyes. I am a teacher. I teach what I most need to learn, and you get to learn right along with me.

I will outline the steps to viewing the world through a perspective of pleasure. As funny as it sounds, we resist pleasure as human beings. We are programmed for negativity, and we need to make an active effort to think positively. This book will help you make that effort become natural and easy. Pleasure is a reconnection with your inner wisdom.

What is here, inside each and every one of us, is a beautiful, sensual and sexual being. There is a crazy perception prevalent in our world that begins with our views on beauty and extends to unhealthy habits and behavior around sex.

Although there is a growing movement toward embracing the curves in a woman's body, we still hold the image of beauty as gorgeous skin, long hair, 5-foot-9, 125 lbs., and great teeth. Because the media bombards us with these images, we compare ourselves to this definition of beauty, and that creates the beauty gap – the difference between what we see in the mirror and what we see on the cover of magazines. What is the impact of that?

- Among children in grades 1-3, 42% want to be thinner
- Among 11- to 13-year-old girls, more than 50% believe they are overweight
- More than 10% of teenage girls report binge eating at least once a week
- More than 90% of college women in the mid-1990s had attempted to control their weight through diets
- 80% of U.S. women do not like how they look
- Approximately 1 in 100 women in the U.S. binge and purge in order to lose weight

We also perceive sexuality, one of the most natural parts of being a human being, in a multitude of unhealthy ways. This is very detrimental to our world. Women are unable to relax, allow and receive pleasure. Men are frustrated, and some turn to porn and prostitutes. It's not a good recipe for peace and love, besides the fact we lose all that wonderful feminine energy.

This book is based on my own personal experiences, along with case studies from a special coaching project designed to document my process. It includes my insights from 20 years of leading groups and listening to the frustrations of women's and men's sexual needs not being met. It is a beautiful thing when we begin to open up to discuss these intimate parts of our lives. The room comes alive!

In addition, I have interviewed experts in sexuality, wellness and beauty for my internet radio show. I will share some of the gems from over 150 podcast interviews with people like authors John Gray, Jill Bolte Taylor and Louann Brizendine. I also went on a special project where I spent the summer of 2010 in Europe, traveling and interviewing musicians about the healing power of music.

The journey I went on to make the discoveries and learn the lessons that I've included in this book took at least 26 years, almost half my life. It was a deep, soulful journey, and a path that only I could travel. As I learned and taught what I learned, and then learned some more, the process of how to integrate the feelings of peace, passion and pleasure became more clear to me.

As you read and absorb the simple concepts from this book and practice the basic, yet profound exercises offered, you will feel the gentle invitation to slow down and begin to enjoy your life more. You will have more clarity about your pleasure and then be able to channel pleasure energy to ordinary experiences.

Imagine using the sexual healing vibration for doing the dishes or sitting with your child during homework. Your energy will increase, and you will bring a light and fun energy to everyone lucky enough to be in your world. Loving yourself and becoming free from judgment is another great outcome of opening to the pleasure perspective.

The three-step process of experiencing more peace, passion and pleasure is:

1) PAUSE
2) PONDER
3) PULSE

They are separate steps that warrant an entire book of their own (available in digital form on Amazon), so you will find a section devoted to each of these steps within this book.

In the first section on PAUSE, I write about when you stop and get off the vicious cycle, then you're able to feel your feelings rise to the surface. Those feelings are your inner knowing, your inner wisdom and your truth.

Once they rise to the surface to contemplate, meditate or PONDER, it allows you to make conscious and mindful choices based on what you want. When you are not afraid to look inside and face whatever you find there, then you are free – free to be who your soul is crying for you to be; free to be who the world needs you to be.

My experience is that many people understand the value of contemplation and meditation, and yet don't know how to integrate the benefits of what they've learned or even see what they've learned from these practices. Any expectation of what you are supposed to see outweighs the good ah-ha's of what you will find in section 2 on PONDER.

You've PAUSED, you've PONDERED, and your ability to experience pleasure in your body is heightened after reading the first two sections. The third and final section on PULSE will cap the inward journey and encourage you to express outwardly a release of the positive vibrations of pleasure. When those vibrations reach a tipping point, there will be a global healing.

That is why I wrote this book. I know we can create a much safer and happier planet, and I want to make my contribution to this world healing.

To PULSE magnificence into the world is to contribute your own unique positive vibration to the whole, which has an impact far beyond your wildest imagination. You can affect people with your nonverbal vibrational energy as much, if not more, than you can with your words. Becoming aware of your nonverbal energy involves living in your body, not your analytical mind.

I wrote this book to give you easy-to-follow concepts and simple exercises that may require 15 to 20 minutes of your time to explore your inner wisdom and truth. When you come out the other side, you will know how to take a deeper look at who you really are.

It was fascinating for me to learn why we resist being present in our experience and trusting our inner truths. We have been trained through organized religion, politics, health care, and other systems of which we have little control, to trust others before we trust ourselves.

What are some of the repercussions of this phenomenon in our world?

- Low self-esteem and self-worth
- Women set themselves up for failure by comparing their bodies to models on magazine covers (the average U.S. woman is 5-foot-4 and weighs 140 lbs., while the average model is 5-11 and weighs 117 lbs.)
- We have a happiness deficit because we don't feel good in our own skin
- Women have a difficult time feeling sexual and being present with their partners because they are too worried about how they look naked
- Women have a difficult time achieving orgasm
- Men don't understand women's body issues and don't know how to help
- Women wait until men find them attractive

- Women relinquish their natural role in choosing mates

These repercussions have a huge negative impact on our planet. If women do not feel happy with their bodies, they do not find their relationships fulfilling and satisfying. It is hard for a man to feel happy when a woman feels inadequate and unhappy about the way she looks. When women are feeling their beauty and sexuality, they can literally breathe with the earth.

How can we bring the beauty back? How can we encourage our children to look within to their beautiful souls for how they feel, and not their outer appearance? What is the role of the woman in this journey back? What is the role of the man?
I invite women to BE thankful for your body and how it has served you throughout your life: the pleasures, the pains, the glories, the defeats. Feel grateful for ALL of it, as all of your experiences have led you to this point in your life.

And I invite all mindful men to appreciate something about your own body, and then extend that to appreciate something about a woman's body. Maybe say, "Honey, you look really beautiful today." Simple, yet so powerful.

A woman who loves her body PULSES one of the most beautiful energy vibrations on the planet, and her children are watching and learning!

What you learn in this book will make sense to you, because you already know it deep inside.

Coach Betty

Part 1

PAUSE

Chapter 1

The Day That Marvin Gaye Spoke to Me

I have a fascinating story to share with you. It involves my experience of a deep emotional physical pain that literally ripped open my life and changed its course forever. There was a dramatic transformation that took place, and it started with a very simple concept. Simple in our world today, but not always easy. It started with a PAUSE.

Here is how it works. Feel your feet on the floor. Take a deep breath. Imagine yourself slowing down and becoming more aware of all your surroundings. Take another breath. That is the basics of "The Powerful PAUSE." We must PAUSE so we can experience more pleasure.

Let me tell you how I learned about "The Powerful PAUSE."

I was diagnosed with a chronic pain condition 26 years ago. Prior to that, I was an extreme athlete. In my twenties, I hiked up Mount Whitney and other peaks, took long distance bike rides, and earned a Bachelor of Arts degree in dance. I loved to move. It was what brought me to life and made me feel good. My dream was to help other people get in their bodies and feel good.

Well, the universe had other plans for me.

One day I woke up, and as soon as I lifted the covers off and felt pain radiating down my arm, I knew something terrifying was going on in my body. Everywhere in my body – shoulders, elbows, wrists, hips, knees, ankles, and fingers – was searing in pain. I could not even begin to close my fingers. It felt like I had a claw for a hand.

Standing up, I walked like a robot down the hall to the bathroom and sat on the toilet, unsure whether I would be able to get up by myself. And slightly more terrified than me was my husband, at the time. Poor guy, he was a hypochondriac already. He was white with fear as he watched me wince in pain walking down the hallway. We had climbed Mount Whitney less than a year earlier. He was as baffled as I was, but with a much more pessimistic view of the future. He thought I would end up in a wheelchair.

Although he was a saint in those first few years, what's referred to as the "chronic long-haul" was too painful for him. It's understandable, really. I was cycling and cycling and not getting to any real healing. It's hard to watch someone you love do that. The name of this condition is rheumatoid arthritis (RA). There are many different forms of arthritis, and RA is characterized by hot, swollen painful joints all over the body. It's not specific to any one joint.

I remember driving my daughter to her activities with my hands on the steering wheel. It was frightening to watch my knuckles become deformed before my eyes. Only crippled people look like this. My dance career took a big PAUSE as I was unable to look in a full-length mirror for 16 years.

Managing my own emotions was dicey, to say the least. Now, my husband was freaking out wondering where the active woman he married went. Would she ever come back? I was trying to take care of him, at the cost of my own health. The marriage began to unravel.

Now you all know some experience of pain. You've cut your fingers, had sprains, broken bones or a headache. Imagine that pain to be all over your body and its duration longer than you think you can handle. How long would you be able to tolerate it when people are telling you to do things that don't work, and yet they just keep telling you to do the same thing over and over?

I know this part of my story is not fun to hear, but what if I told you the pleasure is right next door to the pain? What if I told you, just be in the possibility of it, that there is something that is not widely talked about that could take you from that pain to pleasure? How long would you go before you would try it?

What I have discovered over the last 26 years is the realization that we carry pleasure with us wherever we go, and it is a powerful force for healing.

I want you to hold onto two possibilities:

1) You can move from pain to pleasure by learning to access your inner wisdom which results in organic and orgasmic living
2) Sex, laughter, beauty, joy all have healing powers

Orgasms have been used in healing since the beginning of time. It is documented in the 1880s that Victorian physicians used vaginal massage for the diagnosis of female hysteria. The movie "Hysteria", based on true events, documents it. This practice led to the invention of the vibrator. Wikipedia lists this is the fifth domestic use of electricity.

Think of how good an orgasm feels (if you are one of the lucky women who know the feeling). What if that feeling was like a pill you took for relief? I have been going to doctors for a long time. Pills are offered to ease the pain today, while back in the day, they handed out vibrators.

What if I told you that relaxing into an orgasm would be like taking a 20-minute pill?

This book is not a promise for a new kind of cure for pain, only a promise that we can feel much better living in our bodies, health condition or not. It is absolutely possible to feel the flow of life and have ecstatic experiences, no matter what your circumstances. Audrey Hepburn said it best:

"Nothing is impossible. The word itself says I'm possible."

As I said, I was an extreme athlete prior to this diagnosis. I had few health concerns growing up. Initially I went to the doctor and said, "Just tell me what to do so I can go back to my life." This had always worked in the past. For a condition like RA, the primary prescription was pharmaceutical medication to control inflammation and pain. The drugs would work for a while, and then a flare would break through and the doctor would put me on a higher dosage or add a new drug. It felt like a vicious cycle.

I want to PAUSE right here and say I have nothing against pharmaceutical medications. The drugs allowed me to pick up my baby and be involved in her life.

I didn't rely on drugs alone. I researched and read voraciously about self-management of pain. I learned about something called self-efficacy, which means one's confidence in one's ability to make changes. It was a turning point and helped define my career path. I became a Master Trainer for the Stanford Self Efficacy Program, and traveled throughout the San Francisco Bay Area speaking and teaching courses.

The bottom line of self-efficacy is if you believe you have the confidence to change, you do have the confidence. Henry Ford is quoted as saying "Whether you think you can or your can't, you're usually right." PAUSE on that one.

So for the next 15 years, I continued to take medications and teach people about self-efficacy.

Then two events happened that changed the road I was on. One was my daughter turned 16 and was able to drive herself to school, work and get around independently. This happened at the same time that a medication I had been taking for eight years, Celebrex, was found to cause deaths. When the Food and Drug Administration (FDA) first approved this drug, it was considered the latest greatest medical discovery. My physician said, "I'm putting all my patients on this drug. It's the greatest thing since sliced bread." After the reports of the fatalities, I returned to his office and he emphatically said he was taking all patients off this drug. At that moment, I felt there just had to be a better way.

I asked him to help me safely taper off all the medication I was taking. He did not agree with my decision to go off all medication, but my inner wisdom voice spoke louder and more firmly. It was a radical step, as it ended a relationship with the person who had been directing my health care for 12 years. I felt empowered. I knew I could do what I needed to do, but it felt lonely. It was me and my inner guide on this part of the journey. That was over eight years ago. It felt amazing to get off pharmaceuticals. I heard myself saying, "I feel alive again." Some of that being alive was very painful.

It was about two months after stopping all drugs that my body was in shock. I was now dealing with pain that has been masked for the last 15 years. Turning over in bed was a major ordeal. It took all morning, with baths, rest and slow exercises, to feel ready to climb the stairs and start my day.

While there are many different ways to respond to this kind of deep pain, I am an optimist at my core. My dad was the ultimate optimist, and I know I inherited his gene for this. My dad used to believe the Chicago Cubs would win the World Series in his lifetime. In case you aren't an American baseball fan, the Cubs are considered "lovable losers," because their fans support them despite the fact they haven't won a World Series in more than a hundred years.

I'm very good at being optimistic. My friends and clients who come to me, know I will challenge their negative thinking. I provide encouragement when people are at the end of their rope. It's why I am Coach Betty.

So I chose to respond to my new pain challenge by opening my mind to possibilities. My training as a life coach and a master trainer for the classes at Stanford set me up perfectly for this. One afternoon, I was lying in bed with pain at a level 10 on a scale of 1 to 10. My entire body was throbbing, and I felt pain where I didn't know I had joints. I was still clear and committed to a different path. So I surrendered to the pain and allowed whatever feelings and thoughts to come through. I was in the biggest PAUSE I have ever been in my life. My body was in PAUSE, and my mind was active and calm. This was what I begin to hear:

Marvin Gaye singing..."And when I get that feeling I want sexual healing..."

Marvin Gaye is an American singer-songwriter and musician. His Grammy Award-winning 1982 hit "Sexual Healing" is on the 500 greatest songs of all time. This song is also considered the number 1 song to "get you in the mood" for sex.

So it started running through my mind. Wow, I begin thinking this would be an amazing time to experiment with sexual healing, given all this pain. So I did just what Marvin Gaye suggested. I had a courageous and supportive partner who was completely and utterly safe. I called him up and invited him to participate in a sexual healing experiment. Now, I hadn't had sex in six months as I was getting off the medication. It took special handling, with lots of gentleness and kindness, to have sexual intercourse with me. We made love all night long. He was so tender and gentle that I was able to relax into multiple orgasms and release after release. It was a night I will never forget. The next morning I stood up and walked down the hall with ease, pain level at 3.

No, I do not have the privilege to give you his phone number. If you don't have anyone in your life like that, there are many safe and loving ways to activate healing sex and healing orgasms. That is why I was compelled to write this series of books on Pleasure Medicine.

After this experience, I realized that Marvin really has been singing about something powerful all these years. Coming from the conservative Midwest, you might imagine this was not discussed at my dinner table. We were talking about how the Cubs never should have traded future Hall of Famer Lou Brock to the rival St. Louis Cardinals.

I had to start from scratch to research and learn. I couldn't go to the parents for this one. I became familiar with Tantric sexual energy and Kundalini energy. I am not an expert in either one of these modalities. What I set out to do was understand the subject of orgasmic energy healing and how it works for easing pain. I studied and learned from some of the best teachers.

I discovered and learned how to become acutely aware of orgasmic energy and how to channel it for pain relief. As I continued to explore and experiment with this energy, I also was able to channel it into ordinary experiences. I would find it orgasmic to listen to my daughter read from her poetry journal, and I would take celebration in drinking a cup of coffee and listening to the birds. Cooking dinner made my senses come alive. Experiences I used to take for granted now were ecstatic experiences.

I'm not talking about having orgasms at the stove or in restaurants, like the scene from "When Harry Met Sally." I'm talking about following the flow of life, listening to the wisdom of your body and squeezing the juice out of every moment. When you are living your life from this place, then your sex life also can be ecstatic.

PAUSE. Put your hand on your lower belly. Breathe deep down into that belly right underneath your hands. Let me plant the seed that there is a fountain of healing juice that lives right there when you get really quiet with yourself. You can use this healing juice to transform ordinary experiences into extraordinary moments. It is a path of creativity and freedom, as well as making you feel younger and more youthful. Having fun with mundane tasks, like cleaning the house or doing homework with your child, can become moments of pleasure as you sit with a new presence.

What would it take for you to open your mind and water that seed of possibility?

I'm on a mission to reconnect women with their beauty and sexuality. It is our birthright and one of the gifts we bring to the planet. When women feel beautiful and sexual, everybody wins. The problem is that only 3 percent of women worldwide call themselves beautiful, and at least 43 percent of women have difficulty achieving orgasm.

Does that make you as sad as it makes me? Think of all that yummy feminine energy that gets lost because women don't really feel good about how they look, and they have a hard time allowing, receiving and surrendering to pleasure.

What kind of relationship do you have with your body? Is it loving? Is it kind? There were times I was so pissed off at my body. I would swear at my knees and cry at my elbows. You have a relationship with your body, and you listen to your body. That's what we do when we're hungry, thirsty and tired. What I want to do is improve your awareness and increase your sensitivity to the messages your body is giving you, and then increase them to pleasurable sensations. This creates what I call an organic and orgasmic life.

THE PROCESS

Here is the secret of how to fall in love with yourself in three simple steps. I call it the 3 Ps to peace, passion and pleasure.

1 - PAUSE. It's simple, but not always easy. We need to get off the hamster wheel. We need to breathe more. We need to accept where we are in life without judgment.

2 - PONDER. We need to reconnect with our core values and what is meaningful in life.

3 - PULSE. We practice PAUSING, PONDERING, and making choices that honor our core values and what is important to us. Then we create a new rhythm to live by that is our unique dance. We are worth it!

Rx from Chapter 1

1) Mirror work: Every morning before you leave the house, look in the mirror and take at least 30 seconds to connect with your own eyes. No matter what challenges you may be experiencing right now, you are lovable. You are doing enough. Practice this until you really believe it. Others will never be able to fill what you do not fill for yourself.

2) Sensuality breaks: Become aware of your five senses of sight, sound, smell, taste and touch. Take at least 30 seconds a day to become completely absorbed in one of those senses. For example, buy a gardenia and place it in a bowl next to your bed. Every night when you get in bed, take 30 seconds before you go to sleep to focus and enjoy the fragrance. It doesn't hurt to smile while you do.

In Chapter 2, John Gray and some other amazing guests from my radio show will share their wisdom on the importance and benefits of taking a PAUSE.

Chapter 2

PAUSE: The Main Ingredient in the Pleasure Prescription

PAUSE is essential to truly experiencing pleasure. Have you had the experience where you were so excited about some event, and the day of the event came and you were so busy making sure everything was running smoothly that you didn't really experience the event at all?

I have a cousin who would go on vacation with her family, and she spent the vacation time taking care of all of the logistics and it wasn't until she returned home that she was actually able to enjoy what they had done on their vacation. She was not able to experience the pleasure of the moment because she was too busy making sure all was okay.

It is an out-of-body experience to postpone your feelings until later. When we feel the joy and pleasure as it is happening, the feeling is enhanced. To have fulfilling sex, you cannot postpone being in your body until a later time. That is true for all of our life experiences. Being present within the moment is so important, and I will explore it more deeply with you later in this book.

The PAUSE I took in Chapter 1 was demanded by my body. When I reflect back on it, it was as if my body was saying "Stop, and pay attention here!" Because of my choice to get off all medications and allow my body to feel the underlying pain that was very real, it created a PAUSE where I could not move without an enormous amount of pain. It was directed by my body and not my mind. I could not override the messages that my body was giving me at that point in time. And I realized that this feeling of not being able to override was something different for me. I was listening to my body in a different way.

I learned that this PAUSE principle is so essential to pleasure, that nothing else will make sense until the PAUSE is truly integrated into your life. The three main points I want you to walk away with about PAUSE are:

1) The hamster wheel is not a way to live your life
2) Even the briefest PAUSE can make a big difference
3) The benefits for PAUSING far outweigh the risks

That may sound funny, but often we are afraid to stop and feel. Don't be afraid to stop.

The Hamster Wheel

The vicious cycle of the hamster wheel just do not jive with the experience of pleasure. How can you feel pleasure when your heart is racing, your mind is occupied with a multitude of thoughts, and there is no time to notice what is around you?

We have beauty all around us. When we notice beauty, it creates a moment of pleasure. And in that moment of pleasure, there is a relaxation, a moment of checking in with your body. Even if it is just to smell the flowers, listen to the birds, or feast your eyes on a sunset. What is possible when we learn to PAUSE and enjoy pleasure? What is possible is that you can feel peace. You can tap into the juiciness of passion. It brings a smile to your face. And when you smile, you bring a delightful person to your relationships. What is more fun than a being with a happy person? I know this – and John Gray agrees with me – when we have happy people on our planet, then we have a happy planet. In my interview with John, he had a special message for women:

> *Excerpt from Interview with John Gray on "Green Think Radio", December, 2011*
>
> **John Gray** is an American relationship counselor, lecturer and author. In 1992 he published the book "Men Are from Mars, Women Are from Venus", which became a long-term bestseller and formed the central theme of all his subsequent books and career activities. His books have been bought by millions of people around the world, while drawing criticism from academics for trivializing the dynamics of relationship psychology. His first book has sold more than 7 million copies, and according to a 1997 report by the book's publisher, HarperCollins, is the all-time, bestselling, hardcover nonfiction book.

Coach Betty Louise: How do you connect understanding each other in relationships to helping to heal our planet?

John Gray: I think there is a parallel going on in the world right now, with the global warming and the problems of the planet: the devastation of the planet, the disrespect of the planet, the dishonoring of the planet. And it is Mother Earth, it's the feminine principle. And what has been going on for the last 20 years is that, although on one level, there have been huge advances for women in terms of equal opportunity, equal pay, and this whole movement is a great thing. But at the same time, in order to make that transition and make that shift, women have, to a great extent, given up a lot of the nurturing activities that they used to do; and as a result, women are more stressed and more unhappy than ever before.

You can actually go back to some indigenous countries on the planet right now, and you'll see that women are much, much happier than women today (in the US). But if we just go back 30 years and look at the psychological tests from universities, we see that women's level of happiness has significantly dropped. You can measure this physiologically by the stress hormone, cortisol. Cortisol levels in women have dramatically gone up. The average working woman has twice the cortisol of the average working man. When a man comes home from work, he has a chance to relax and let his cortisol levels drop and restore balance to his system. For women, when they get home, those cortisol levels double. This is a major factor. It is just happening since the 80s, and of course this is really where global warming just happened as well.

This is played out physiologically in tests. The fact that one out of three women are on anti-depressants or sleeping pills, which are examples of high levels of stress. Adrenal fatigue is responsible for all the menopausal symptoms women are experiencing today. I'm not saying men don't experience this increasing stress, but women are experiencing it much higher than men. This takes a huge toll on relationships, and of course it takes a huge toll on women. But it is a metaphor as well. If we are not tending toward women's needs, we are not tending toward the needs of the planet.

Women have essentially lost knowledge of what it takes to make them happy.

Where do we find our happiness again? In the PAUSE.

Every little PAUSE counts

This is a simple concept. Why is it so hard for us to be simple? We live in a complicated world. Just look at our government. I could tell you some stories about paperwork and Social Security. You do not have to look far to see how complicated we make things. Another example of how we complicate things is our healthcare system. To keep things simple actually takes a conscious effort.

That is why I want to let you know this is not about learning how to sit in the lotus position and meditate for an hour or even 10 minutes. As I pointed out in chapter 1, 30 seconds of pausing and breathing can make a tremendous difference in how relaxed you are throughout your day. My experiments with clients have been to give them homework of PAUSING for 30 seconds three times a day. That is one and a half minutes of your time. I want to challenge anyone that tells me they don't have 90 seconds in their day to improve their health and increase their pleasure.

The hardest part is in the remembering, so tying it to something you do every day is essential. Consider these options: stop for 30 seconds before each meal or when you wake up, have lunch, go to bed.

Benefits Outweigh the Risks

What are the benefits of PAUSING? When we stop and listen to the messages and wisdom of our body, we get clarity about what is true for us. We have the opportunity when we PAUSE to respond and not react. What do I mean by that? There is a subtle difference between responding and reacting. The connotation for reacting implies less thought. My definition of responding is to answer in a calm and careful way. When we have more clarity, and we are in a calm and careful state of mind, inner peace is more available to us and those around us.

The risks are that you will PAUSE and feel something you don't want to feel. Something that doesn't feel good. It is important to pay complete attention to what you are thinking, and how you feel about that. When you feel yourself thinking in language and thinking at a very fast rate so that your body actually accelerates in your heart and your anxiety level goes up, that is when fear and stress show up. You can train yourself to become aware of this sensation in your body. And whenever that happens, you can PAUSE, step back and evaluate. Do I want to choose to continue down this thinking path of the left hemisphere of the brain or should I come back into the slower and more peaceful part of my right brain? It is a choice, and a PAUSE is the key to making the shift.

One of the first interviews on my show "Women on Air" was with the amazing Dr. Jill Bolte Taylor. Dr. Taylor is a brain scientist who had a brain injury that completely shut down the left side of her brain. She is a brain scientist who had a stroke in her brain and understood what was going on at the time. She wrote a fascinating book about the experience, "My Stroke of Insight." What she learned about peace, passion and pleasure made her one of Time Magazine's 100 Most Influential People for 2008. I recommend her TED talk in which she describes what happens during her stroke of insight. It's fascinating!

Rx from Chapter 2

1) Continue the mirror work. Take 30-second sensuality breaks.
2) Explore pausing before reacting to conversations you have with your partner, your children, your colleagues, your friends that rub you the wrong way.

By the time you complete this series of books on pleasure medicine, you will be able to know how you feel, ask for what you want and need, and be able to express yourself clearly.

The next chapter challenges you to focus when you PAUSE. When you do, you can change your world.

Chapter 3

No Multi-Tasking ... Please

In a sociologic study at Michigan State University, Professor Barbara Schneider reports, "When you look at men and women in similar kinds of work situations, they look very similar. But when they come home, it is very clear that women are shouldering much more of the responsibilities of housework and childcare." This supports the notion that women are much more likely to multitask as a way of being, functioning in the world.

I have a dear friend who is a very busy working mom. She came to one of my workshops where I was teaching this concept of PAUSE. She thought it was a really good idea to experiment with, so the next time I saw her she wanted to share how well she was PAUSING. We were in the car and she was driving to her son's soccer game, eating a bagel, and at a stoplight said, "Okay, now I'm going to PAUSE and enjoy this bite of bagel." If it is not clear why this is very funny in terms of implementing my idea of PAUSE, you are probably a busy woman who also functions in the world this way. Consider that she was driving, eating and interacting with me as she was experiencing her PAUSE.

Now I'm sure she did taste that bagel more than she would have had she been driving and talking to me while eating it. To fully get the sensual moment of PAUSING for pleasure, it might have looked like getting to the game, parking, and while her son was warming up, eat the bagel with a minimum of conversation and much more mindful presence.

The first thing to understand about sensuality is that it is impossible to multitask and be sensual. Sensuality is the first step to one of the most natural and fulfilling forms of pleasure we have available to us – sex. Sensuality, of course, is far more than just sex. Our sensuality involves all five senses. Our sensuality is with us 24/7 to see, hear, smell, taste and touch. A moment of sensuality is all about paying attention fully to one of those senses. Sensuality and pleasure go hand-in-hand.

Sensuality Moments in Everyday Life:

- Feeling the sheets on your skin

- Feeling the water stream down your body in the shower

- Smelling the coffee, the eggs, the bacon (breakfast)

- Stopping and visually pausing to look at a beautiful flower, your beautiful child, or your beautiful partner

- Tasting the sip of coffee or the bite of egg

- Listening to one of your favorite songs, dancing if inspired, before starting your day

- Looking at yourself in the mirror and appreciating the unique beauty before you

- Purchasing a fragrant flower, as simple as one gardenia, and placing it in a cup of water next to your bed

- During sex, verbally sharing with your partner how his touch excites you

- Touching your skin lightly and feeling the sensation

Your mindful presence of these sensuality moments is a very simple way to bring more pleasure into your life.

What exactly is mindful presence? Mindful presence is an attentive awareness to what is happening right before you. We often hear the phrase, "being present in the moment," and what that means is to have thoughts and actions focused on what is happening now. Of course, you are always present in your life because you are the one living it. Have you ever driven home and realized that you don't remember the drive. You were a million miles away from what was a routine route, so you allowed your mind to completely drift. How often do you plan your day while lying in bed in the morning?

What would it take to allow the first few minutes of your day to begin with feeling – feeling the sheets, the air, the touch of an animal or a partner, or your own touch to awaken the mindful presence of sensuality?

As a person who has lived with daily pain for many years, I have learned that it is my choice to be attentive to the pain or attentive to the pleasure. They are both available to me always. It is my mind that chooses where to focus. Even though I have of painful condition in my body made worse through movement, when I get into bed at night and relax my entire muscular and skeletal structure, I am often free of pain. Those, for me, are moments of ecstatic pleasure.

There is a segment I do on my radio show called Whoa Babies. Whoa Babies are sound bites that I have read or heard that make me stop and consider the impact on the world. Sometimes Whoa Babies are things to consider integrating into our lives. And sometimes they are things to consider eliminating from our lives. Sometimes what I read literally makes me say, "Whoa Baby." Let me share a Whoa Baby with you from a guest I interviewed, Dr. Louann Brizendine, author of two books: "The Female Brain" and "The Male Brain." Here is what Dr. Brizendine had to say about what needs to happen in our brain before we can enjoy the pleasure of our orgasms.

"Female sexual turn-on begins, ironically, with a brain turn off. The impulses can rush to the pleasure centers and trigger an orgasm only if the amygdala – the fear and anxiety center of the brain – has been deactivated. Before the amygdala has turned off, any last-minute worry about work, the kids or schedules can interrupt the march toward orgasm. The fact that women require this extra neurological step may account for why it takes her on average 3 to 10 times longer than the typical male to reach orgasm."

PAUSING and bringing this mindful presence to your day-to-day activities allows you to enjoy a calm awareness of your body, mind and spirit. This is an easy thing to say and not such an easy thing to do. If it was easy, there wouldn't be a need for this book.

I, along with many other mindful leaders, want to continue to build momentum for the movement toward increased sensuality, sexuality and beauty in our lives so that calm awareness of our body, mind and spirit can create an inner peace, an inner joy.

When we have satisfied men and women enjoying a feeling of inner peace, the peace can extend to neighborhoods, communities, cities, states, countries and encircle the world. Imagine your life feeling peaceful, calm, passionate and pleasurable no matter what your circumstances. You could extend that energy to your family, your neighborhood, your community, your state and your world. Everyone who is lucky enough to be in your presence would be influenced by that inner peace. Imagine that.

John Lennon said it best.

Imagine there's no heaven
It's easy if you try
No hell below us
Above us only sky
Imagine all the people living for today

Imagine there's no countries
It isn't hard to do
Nothing to kill or die for
And no religion too
Imagine all the people living life in peace

You, you may say
I'm a dreamer, but I'm not the only one
I hope someday you'll join us
And the world will be as one

Imagine no possessions
I wonder if you can
No need for greed or hunger
A brotherhood of man
Imagine all the people sharing all the world

You, you may say
I'm a dreamer, but I'm not the only one
I hope someday you'll join us
And the world will live as one

Rx from Chapter 3

1) Choose from the list of mindful moments of sensuality and pick three. During your 30 seconds of pause, three times a day notice one of those five senses wherever you happen to be.

2) During those sensuality moments, become aware of your gut, your solar plexus and lower belly (the second and third chakra areas), and become mindfully present and attentive to what you feel there. Is it tense, calm, butterfly-ish, tight, relaxed, etc? Record the results in your journal.

The next chapter expands on the sensuality of PAUSE. It's juicy!

Chapter 4

Ask for What You Want and Need

I became aware of this concept in an intensive leadership program. The actual phrase we learned and practiced during this eight-month intensive was, "Ask for what you want and need 100 percent of the time, and then stick around and negotiate." What we do so often is work with the needs of others instead of paying attention to our own needs. I know this habit well.

There was a moment in my life when I was asked, "What do you want, Betty"? And I didn't have a clue of what I wanted in that moment. My life seemed to exist to take care of my aging mother, my three-year-old daughter, my working husband, to name a few. Yes, I was a co-dependent extraordinaire. It was the role that was very familiar for me. So second nature, that I was in my fifties before I realized fully what was going on. I humbly say "fully," as there's always more to learn.

This is our history. In the 1950s after World War II, many women in the U.S. stopped working for the war effort, married soldiers coming back from the war and started families. That was my mother. She married my father in 1942, and never worked a day of her life for compensation after that. My prideful father thought that was the best way to support and take care of her. Many women were happy staying home.

The underlying consequence was that these women communicated with children all day and lost touch with other women. And when we lost touch with other women, we stopped collaborating and creatively working together for community. The characteristic of collaboration is very powerful for women. It has been shown that a meaningful conversation between women raises their oxytocin levels (the pleasure hormone). Instead, we moved towards a masculine-based world and a competitive-based society. Women were dumbed down and self-esteem was sinking, so we fell into the masculine, competitive way of being.

In the 1970s, women even wore shoulder pads, which made them look even more masculine. In today's world, I don't know that men have it easy at all. Many women act like men in women's bodies. To survive in the business corporate worlds, shutting down sexuality is necessary. Catharine Hakim, author of the book "Honey Money," writes that women have missed an opportunity to use their erotic capital in the business world.

She claims we wouldn't have these pay discrepancies between men and women if women could embrace their erotic capital and use it wisely. Women are sensual and sexual beings. Women carry the ability to bring beauty to the world and vibrate beauty out into the world in a way that is unique and wonderful. What would change if we were conscious of this truth, and also learned to ask for what we want and need?

Nicole Daedone is a woman speaking around the world about women and orgasms. I had lunch with one of her top staff people one day in San Francisco, headquarters for Nicole's organization, OneTaste. Rachel Cherwitz is originally from Texas, and while growing up had had an eating disorder. She moved to San Francisco in her mid-20s and was drawn to OneTaste.

Rachel learned the practice of orgasmic meditation, a 15-minute stroking meditation where women are brought to orgasm. During this 15 minutes of stroking, women learn to tell their stroker what feels good and where to move their finger to create more sensation. As Rachel practiced this, through specific communication skills taught by OneTaste, she learned to ask for what she wanted and needed in other areas of her life. Her anorexia was cured.

I could write an entire book on communication skills, and someday maybe I will, but for now what I want you to know is the main variables in communication are the words you choose, the tone of your voice, and the geography of your body. Be kind when you are asking for what you want and need.

I am excited about the new conversations that are being started around women's sexual fulfillment with people like Nicole. Women have shortchanged themselves in this area for a variety of reasons that don't really matter anymore. We all deserve sexual satisfaction and fulfillment, and women are stepping up to go for it. It will ultimately make the planet a more peaceful place. Why is it important to write books like this and have these conversations for the sake of women? This Whoa Baby will explain why.

> "According to Semprae Laboratories in 2009, 43 percent of women were sexually dissatisfied. That number is almost half of the women in the world who make up more than half of the population. So we are talking about a lot of dissatisfaction on a very innate, core level. We are sexual beings. It is one of the reasons we are out of balance in our world, we are not taking care of ourselves. We need to feel love and happiness inside before we can have healthy relationships."

> My interview with the co-founder and former president of Semprae Laboratories, Rachel Braun Scherl, reveals some insights into what is going on.

> "There is a huge number of women with a unmet need. When we talked to physicians, we found that only 3 to 5 percent of gynecologists and obstetricians, doctors focused on women and sexuality, have conversations with their patients about sexual satisfaction. They talk about fertility, they talk about sexual health, but they don't talk about satisfaction."

Has your doctor brought this subject up with you? Asking our doctors for what we want and need, and starting these conversations is each and every woman's responsibility. You deserve to be satisfied and it is good for the planet.

Creating a new frame around how we view sex and our sexuality can help make the conversations easier. Here is an excerpt from an interview I had with Veronica Monet. As a Certified Sexologist, and Couples Consultant, Veronica provides her clients with a Shame Free Zone where sex is considered a normal, natural part of life.

> "Sex does not have to be in this little ghetto. Most of us see sex as this dark and dirty thing, and it's over here in the

corner. My holistic approach to sex is that sex is the only reason you are breathing air; it is why you are alive. For most of us, somebody had sex in order to create us. And that points to the central importance of our sex lives. I'm trying to expand our view of sex. If sex is spring and sex is flowers, and women have orgasms when they're in natural childbirth and breastfeeding their babies, then sex is a central part of life."

Rx from Chapter 4

1) During your PAUSEs throughout the day, ask yourself, "What do I want and need in this moment?"

2) Prepare and PRACTICE how you will express this to others. Look in the mirror, and practice the words and tone. Feel what kindness looks like on you.

- "Honey, what I want and need from you right now is..."

- "... is what would make me very happy right now."

- "My request is for ... to happen."

- "Oh Baby, I love your touch, and if you would ... I will be in ecstasy!"

Now, let's add in a sprinkle of more pleasure by increasing our awareness and focus on positivity in Chapter 5.

Chapter 5

Notice What Works Well

"Eighty percent of what you tell yourself you believe." This quote is from my radio guest, Marci Lock. Marci is president of MarciLock.com and Everlasting Fitness. Her story of losing 70 pounds in three months with results lasting more than four years ago has motivated her to become a transformational coach. She speaks and teaches her clients how to change their self-talk to boost positive beliefs. When you notice what is working in your life, your belief system changes right along with it.

What is your self-talk? Are you telling yourself your life is fun, adventurous, and joyful? Or do you hear yourself say that life is hard, a struggle, and a pain in the you-know-where? The tricky part is that sometimes this voice is buried deeply and we are not even conscious of it. Another one of my wonderful radio guests, Dr. Rick Hansen, wrote a book called "Buddha Brain: The Practical Neuroscience of Happiness, Love and Wisdom." He explains why we need to be aware of our self-talk. Our brains are wired for negativity, and we actually need to make an active effort to think positively.

> "What modern science is enabling us to do, which is fantastic and unprecedented because this has never happened before in human history. By neuroscientists peering into the brain, we are starting to understand the circuits of that happiness, love and wisdom so skillfully that we can light up those circuits ourselves. And the way the brain works is when you light up circuits, you actually strengthen them. There is a saying in neuroscience that 'neurons that fire together, wire together.' So by stimulating the neuro basis of happiness, love and wisdom, you strengthen it so you

become centered there and feel increasingly happy, resilient, confident and caring for others."

He goes on to say that PAUSING for 30 seconds and actively focusing on positive things will help rewire the circuit of happiness, love and wisdom. I loved that he said 30 seconds – such a reinforcement for how things don't take hours to process.

My experience is that most people are fear-based, and I blame the media for this. That's why I am part of the movement toward new and more positive media. I encourage you to join me here, because as we get positive input in places where negative images, news stories, and information reign supreme, we will be able to create more positive self-health, attract healthier relationships and care for a healthier planet.

The philosophy on the law of attraction, simply put, is that our thoughts create our life. Mind-body medicine is scientifically documented, and we have yet to explore its full potential for healing miracles. PAUSE is necessary for us to master and recognize our thoughts. Once we become aware of our thoughts, we begin to hear the deeper voices.

My friend, Gerald, shared a childhood story with me that illustrates this point with nature. He used to go down by the river and sit quietly communing with the insects and bugs. He said the longer he quietly sat there, the more different kinds of creatures would appear until he found himself surrounded by spiders, frogs, ants, etc. People who commit to silent meditation retreats will have the experience of more and more inner wisdom being revealed as the days of quiet go by. As you PULSE with the 30-second PAUSEs, you will become proficient at accessing the deeper voices.

I will be going into positivity in great detail in the next book in the series, "Healing with Pleasure Medicine: PONDER." For now, I want you to PULSE with being grateful for simple things. One of the gifts in having had rheumatoid arthritis for 26 years is I have come to appreciate simple things that I used to take for granted. I'm talking about things like lifting the covers off me in the morning, brushing my hair, or putting my socks on during pain-free days.

The other thing I have noticed is my journal writing has changed dramatically. I used to write about all the sadness that I needed to process. It would make a great country song, I'm sure, to go through my journals loaded with dramas and traumas. So what I've learned on this path of positivity is to keep gratitude journals. I keep journals about all my victories. Writing about what's working well, talking about what's working well, and thinking about what's working well creates the intention for things to work well; and then it's hard not to manifest things working well.

To be totally honest with you here, I have had a few days in the last few years when finding something in my life that felt like it was working well was very difficult. So I'm not here to say that your goal should be a life perfectly pleasurable 24/7. Choosing the way of pleasure is the consciousness I live in, and I have been able to find moments of pleasure even when I am experiencing pain off the charts. We need some pain to contrast with pleasure and appreciate painless pleasure. Allowing yourself to experience the highs and lows creates extraordinary times, as long as you come back to PULSE with noticing what works well.

Now that we have heightened your awareness for what's working well, let's talk about looking for pleasure in all the right places in Chapter 6.

Rx from Chapter 5

1) PAUSE, and during those 30 seconds, find at least three things that are working well.

2) WRITE down 12 things that went well at the end of the day before you go in bed.

Here is a sample list of mine:

- I'm able to take such a nice deep breath.

- I love the way my bangs fell right on my forehead.

- Feeling fit

- The new lotion is working on my red spots.

- Made a basket throwing a tissue in the trash
- My Chili Relleno casserole was a hit.
- I completed Chapter 5 today.
- My half-hour nap came at just the right time.
- I was able to put the sheets on my bed all by myself.
- I felt sexy and hot in that halter dress.
- My car started and has been so reliable getting me where I need to go.
- I got a new perfect client.

Chapter 6

Looking for Pleasure in all the Right Places

This is going to be a juicy chapter. Get ready to feel the juice and set that as an intention. I promise you it is right there inside of you. To skillfully access the inner juice, one needs to be 100 percent committed to the knowing. PAUSE and notice while you focus your attention on your lower belly and the fountain of juiciness residing there. Enjoy the resulting pleasure.

Your sensuality, sexuality and beauty are available to you everywhere you go. These qualities that we carry within us have many applications outside of the bedroom. Living a juicy life, where you feel vibrant, is how we vibrate sensuality, sexuality and beauty out into the world. Isn't this exciting? Think of the possibilities!

Imagine what kind of world it would be if we were more in touch with this energy that makes us feel good and makes us smile. This series of books is about removing the old, unhealthy views around our sexuality, our sensuality and our beauty. It's really quite criminal that we have so many hang-ups about them. How does it even make sense that the act which brought us all on this planet is considered shameful or something that we should feel guilty about?

This is really a WHOA baby. PAUSE and consider: what is your perspective on your sexuality, sensuality and beauty? Can you look in the mirror and see your beauty? Do you feel like sex and being sensual is a something you shouldn't discuss? To change our views, we need to know where we are now.

Pleasure can sometimes be found in very unusual places. What if I told you that pleasure can be found in rage energy? My interview with Ruth King has some interesting insights into the pleasure of rage.

Ruth King is the author of "Healing Rage: Women Making Inner Peace Possible," and is a respected voice on emotional wisdom. I asked her to explain exactly how she defines emotional wisdom.

> "It's about the union of our intellect and intuition. It's about us having the full experience of our senses without a story. It's about stepping into how we live each moment as if we have no memory, so we can fully be present to the nowness of life. What we are looking at are emotions, which are reflections of fields of liberated energy, and wisdom, which is a state of spaciousness, which is non-solidifying. So there is room to embrace the spaciousness of our lives, the spaciousness of our bodies, rest in our bodies, rest in our skin, rest in the global sense on this planet, becoming fascinated with the details of our lives, and being able to see amazing things in the ordinary."

She believes that women's healing rage will heal our planet globally. We can attend to the world when we recognize that it's a reflection of ourselves, and it's crucial that we do this inner work. Rage energy is raw vibrancy without the story of it. There is great wisdom in our rage when we drop the story. Rage is a doorway to vibrancy within us. Look at rage as pure energy, and then we can mobilize it for pleasure and goodness in life.

I've included Ruth's work in this chapter to pop open your idea about where pleasure exists in your life.

A more obvious place to find pleasure is in our sex life and having orgasms. For an expansive definition of orgasm, I look to my friend, Monica Day, founder of The Sensual Life:

> "Orgasm is the basis of all life. It is the most powerful energy that lives within every single one of us, and between us when we come together in sensual relationships. In popular culture, we have labeled the climax of a sexual experience an "orgasm" – and yet, orgasmic energy is much more expansive, available and abundant than in just these moments. Our ability to feel pleasure, sensation, connection, awareness and love is endless when we enter the gateway of our orgasm."

I have been teaching and talking with women and men about orgasmic healing energy for the last 20 years. Orgasmic healing has been around since the beginning of time, as I mentioned in Chapter 1. When I spoke at a chronic pain support group in the San Francisco Bay Area, a woman shyly raised her hand and asked about how to have sex with all her pain. Most of the other 20 women in the room jumped into the conversation and their experiences. When women feel safe, they come alive when the topic of orgasmic energy and healing comes up. We all went home with big smiles on our faces that night. That's what I'm talking about here – just talking about sex generated orgasmic healing energy for those women.

Orgasms and taboo subjects like domination/submission, S & M, made its way into mainstream media in 2012 when the book "Fifty Shades of Grey" was published. *The Huffington Post* reported that E L James' "Fifty Shades" trilogy has outsold JK Rowling's seven-book Harry Potter series on Amazon's UK site. James has been named the best-selling author of all time at Amazon.co.uk, selling over 40 million copies of "Fifty Shades of Grey" since March 2012. It is the fastest-selling paperback of all time.

It is hard to deny that we love and will spend money on fantasy, whether porn or Potter. This book has been called "Mommy porn" as the fan base is composed largely of married women over 30. Hmm …

Will this improve women's sexual lives? The disturbing and poorly written details would be worth it if that were the outcome.

I have always found graphic descriptions of sexual encounters to be arousing in my body. My first sexual feelings that I remember came from reading "racy" stories in magazines I used to hide under my mattress.

Sex and what arouses a woman is unique to her. The scenes in "Fifty Shades" that created a positive visceral experience for me were when the two main characters expressed love and compassion for each other. Sex without compassion is the lowest form of relationship in my book.

The nature of the dominant/submissive aspect was something that didn't turn me on, but I have no judgment for others as long as the sex is consensual and there is an understanding that there will be pain along with the pleasure. I honestly felt very disturbed that this book was creating such a stir with women. Is it just a deep awakening we desire that sometimes includes pain? Maybe I've just had my share of pain.

Before I explain what I believe may be beneficial about the book, I need to comment on the fantasy man syndrome. The main character, Christian Grey, was the image of the sexiest, richest, smartest and most talented man this side of the North Pole. I want us all to find a way to look past surface glamour and find the true soul. It is not always easy. I fail in this endeavor often.

I found three redeeming thoughts from this odd book.

A sexual relationship requires deep communication. Because of the provocative nature of the sexual requests in this story, verbal communication and speaking your deep truth was repeatedly stressed as necessary. We can all learn from this.

There was also a consciousness about choosing to enter into the relationship because of the extreme nature of the sexual demands. Conscious choosing is a key factor in creating any life you desire.

My final positive takeaway from this book is the encouragement of receptivity. The heroine was showered with gifts that she resisted, until she didn't. There was an air of giving and receiving that took into account value on both sides. It felt natural until it went over the edge of kinkiness for me.

Being the conscious optimist that I am, I invite you to reflect on your own relationships and see where you could:

- communicate your deep truth
- be acutely conscious of your choices
- give and take with love

There is wisdom in all things. It is up to us to find how to make it a pleasurable experience. No one can do that for us.

Learning to embrace our juiciness and express it in the world means we have to PAUSE and evaluate our views, and understand where they come from. My guest, Ina "Laughing Winds" Mlekush, talks about the ancient Mayan and Toltec traditions concerning the healing powers of orgasm and sex.

> Ina teaches Chuluaqui Quodoushka workshops to men and women and says, "Women were trained and learned that their bodies were not theirs. They learned that it was to please the man. Now a lot has taken place since that time.

Women are claiming their sexuality. But we are still very archaic; this country was born from Puritans. So there is still this puritanical view about what is sex and about what is intimacy." Women are still struggling with their boundaries regarding how much sex to have when they are not as motivated as their partners.

Ina goes on to say, "An orgasm a day keeps the doctor away. I don't always feel like making love, but I know it's good for my health. So within five minutes of making love I'm wondering, 'Where did all this sexual energy come from?' All of a sudden, this passion is just burning through me, and five minutes ago I couldn't have cared less."

And then I asked Ina the big question: How can women get over the taboo about self-pleasuring? Her brilliant response: "Well, first of all, if I wait to feel horny or wait to feel beautiful and sexual to self-pleasure, it might never happen because we women have a difficult time seeing our own beauty. So I like to approach it from the other way around. Schedule a time two or three times a week when you can lay in a room on the floor and maybe feel the sun coming through and touching you, and maybe laying nude on the floor, and first gently touch your whole body, awaken your whole body. The genital area for women awakens as our skin awakens. And as you touch yourself, have a little mantra, "I am beautiful and orgasmic." The more we use the 'I am' statement, the more we become it. One of the biggest taboos is to take a mirror and look at yourself; just simply look, and to see that we are a flower. And every flower is different; there is not one that is more beautiful than another."

I look at sun streaming into the room with a whole new attitude since Ina shared this. I just love the simplicity and gentleness of awakening our skin by lying naked in the sun. As I practice sensuality by pausing to feel the sun on my skin, I can become orgasmic all by myself with no one around and not even close to my genitals. I am one of the very lucky women who allows and surrenders to ejaculation.

To me, it is sacred and healing to receive what I consider a gift from the Goddess in me. It is possible for me to become aroused enough to ejaculate during my meditation, anticipating a lover, and any time I surrender to PAUSE, and allow the juiciness to flow. How about that for orgasmic healing pleasure?!

I could write volumes and volumes on where to find pleasure in your body. In your most natural state, you are a sensual being. I trust I have opened your mind to some pleasure possibilities that you may or may not have thought about. I will share more from the work with my clients in the next chapter. Maybe one of their juicy stories will be like yours.

Rx from Chapter 6

1) PAUSE and answer the following two questions for yourself:
    - Can you look in the mirror and see your beauty?
    - Do you believe that sex and sensuality is something you shouldn't openly discuss?
2) Create the intention that you will expand your definition of where you can find pleasure within your own body. Write it down in your journal.

Now let's take a look at how this works in real life situations with a few client case studies.

Chapter 7

Case Studies on the Power of PAUSE

These are actual notes from my client files, with permission from my clients. All of the names have been changed and all of the events are true. These women lived all over the United States: Washington, Michigan, Minnesota, Maryland and West Virginia.

Client Carlene

Carlene is a therapist, 66 years old. In her younger, years she was tormented sexually by others and voluntarily disconnected from her sexuality. Her first orgasm was at age 24. She could see her beauty and felt blessed to have good genes. She married a man who brought her out of a period of darkness, but she has never had an orgasm with him in 25 years. They were a "good managerial couple." She had an extramarital affair with a man for six years where she reconnected with her sexuality. She was longing for an outlet for this rediscovered pleasure. It was very difficult as she developed an aversion to her husband's touch and was torn with thoughts of the erotic affair.

Our work turned her to her relationship with inner sexuality, and understanding the pleasure of her sensuality, sexuality and beauty no matter what. She was quite desperate to have sensual and sexual feelings towards her husband, but felt locked down in her lower belly and wanted the key to unlock the tightness. She wanted to feel liberated from the fear of even bringing up the subject of satisfying sex with her husband.

For two months, she learned the 30-second PAUSE and to feel the sensual and beautiful woman that she is. After two months of pausing, pondering and pulsing with activities like listening to Leonard Cohen songs or the neighborhood frogs that live in her neighborhood, she began to vibrate a new type of energy out in the world.

These were some of the things she noticed changing in her life: the stillness calmed the constant buzz; the stillness allowed her to choose how she wanted to use her energy; the stillness gave her the opportunity to feel grateful, and she felt more connected to a meaningful spirituality.

As she began to embrace her own sensuality again and feel gratitude for the affair instead of guilt, she began to see her husband as a sexual and sensual being. Carlene's courage to address the sexual issue with her husband started with investigating an introductory tantric workshop for them to attend. There were so many other great changes in Carlene's life, like more steadiness, more groundedness, feeling inner peace, and having better boundaries with her children and grandchildren. It inspires me that she made all of these amazing changes at 66 years old. It is never too late to become a sensual and sexual beauty, AND everybody wins when we do.

Client Rebecca

Rebecca is a holistic nurse, 30 years old. She is passionate about teaching healthcare practitioners how to care for themselves. She wanted to be free to express herself sexually and loved the notion of living a juicy life. With the "religious card" a hurdle for her sexual expression, she also felt shut down in her hips and lower belly.

When we would start our calls, I would ask Rebecca some open-ended question about how she was feeling in the moment. Often her response of positive words didn't match up with the tone of her voice. We would dig deeper. "What am I hearing in your voice?" She would PAUSE and admit that she felt drained and exhausted trying to bring her work to the world. She was in a cycle of doing, doing, doing. The great, big fat ah-ha for Rebecca was that pausing in her life, taking time off and experiencing pleasurable activities, was more productive!

I asked her to journal a response to "How productive is rest?" Then I asked her to step away from the computer for 48 hours. She was a committed client and always did her homework. I'm sure she was a straight-A student growing up. She was a star client. After the 48 hours off to replenish, she felt pretty good. But a month later she had cycled back into overwhelm and depletion. She was NOT having fun. Next up was her challenge of taking a month off work and replenishing her soul. She needed a PAUSE to PONDER and figure out what she wanted to do differently so she didn't keep cycling back into this very non-juicy place.

At the end of the month we spoke, and she said she went away and did absolutely nothing. She totally enjoyed herself and wasn't ready to get off her break. It was scary, but she agreed it was necessary. She was writing morning pages from Julia Cameron's "The Artist's Way," and inspirations kept coming. She said, "I wasn't bringing my authentic self forward for the last few years." We talked about what it looks like to be 100 percent Rebecca. She didn't have any clarity on exactly what was next, but she knew what she was doing was not the way to go.

Just two short months later, Rebecca is moving into Reiki energy work and bringing that to western medicine. It is inspiring that she is pursuing what she loves and understands the clarity that comes in the PAUSE. On our last call, she said she is valuing non-doing and sees taking a break as productive. She claimed that my biggest accomplishment with her was to get her to stop. And when she did, she learned to slow down and become more present with herself. She believes she can actually have it all, juicy rest and juicy work. Facebook photos of late reveal that this girl knows pleasure.

Client Nancy

Nancy is a massage therapist, 42 years old. She used to be an erotic dancer and had many sexual experiences through her dancing. She loved the feeling of courage, confidence and grace when she was deeply connected to her sensuality and sexuality. Her dancing really brought her there. But she felt a lot of shame around having gotten there through this time that she was living out on her edges. She was in a very committed relationship with a man and they had great sex.

She had a hard time with her beauty, but knew it was hugely powerful when she was connected with that as well as her sensual, sexual self. She understood that it could contain powerful healing powers and she wanted to tap into it. Her hips were locked and to be able to enjoy the power of her sexuality, she wanted to unlock them.

Are you beginning to see the theme? This is so common for women to have locked hips. Move those hips ladies ... go gentle and easy at first, but loosen them up!

Nancy picked songs to get her move and groove on. I sent her "Sexual Healing" by Marvin Gaye and suggested that she focus on her hips. She said it was rage that needed to be unlocked in her lower chakras. The music was beginning to unlock her inner resistance to expressing the rage. Through movement, she gyrated and shook and even threw in some kicks from martial arts classes. I remember that call. She was so excited. She said, "I can't wipe this grin off my face. I can't wait to come home. I've missed my body. I have a better flow of sexual energy and I am tuned into beauty and grace everywhere." She kept bubbling on, "I have become more flexible and things are working seamlessly."

One of Nancy's physical challenges was hormonal headaches and mood swings. She referred to her particularly moody times as "shark weeks." Her loving partner would often tickle her and stress her out with his rough playing and hugging at these times. The skill of asking for what she wanted and needed 100 percent of the time, and then sticking around to negotiate, proved to be a good solution. She paused, took a breath, and changed the annoyance to, "I just love it when you hug me and play with me. You know I love you. And what I would appreciate from you right now is to help me get lunch on the table so I can make sure I get back to work on time." It was definitely smoother sailing.

The mirror work helped her reach a point where she was satisfied with her shape, and she chose the perspective that it is a journey to be fit and strong. On our last session, she said during a PAUSE she had these thoughts. "I've always had this feeling of not being enough. And then I thought, 'What if I never arrive? What if I never get there?' I need to be in the moment and feel content." I'm fascinated at how we can decide in the moment to PAUSE and BE.

Client Bonnie

Bonnie is a healer who works in the mortgage business, 32 years old. She was happily married, a mom of a beautiful 8-year-old girl. She kept the job in the mortgage business to contribute financially to the family. She knew it wasn't her spiritual calling. She and her husband are in an open relationship, and she has been the driving force behind considering multiple partners. He was resistant and scared, but has agreed to explore it. She made him feel safe by expressing her deep love for him often. She stayed emotionally and physically connected to him by having sex with him up to five times a week. She has a genuine deep appreciation for him, and their marriage and family.

She is a courageous woman who knows how important her sexuality is, and wants to continue to explore the power of it in a deeply spiritual way. She knows her beauty, and men are very attracted to her. She is very conscious of the "altered universe of pleasure from a spiritual place." She has a great desire to help men heal around their sexuality. This is so risky that she hasn't broached the subject with her husband yet. She struggles with remembering to pause regularly. Life is hectic and there always seem to be too much on Bonnie's plate. She lives with chaos. Her first assignment was, "What is good about chaos?"

Bonnie is a dedicated mom. She has anguished over her parenting, trying to be a perfect parent. I point her toward breathing into the humanness of being a parent, pausing, feeling her feet on the ground, and feeling her energy moving down. She now brings her juiciness to her relationship with her daughter. Her young daughter is getting to witness a mom who embraces her beauty and sexiness in a healthy way. She is a very lucky girl.

She comes alive when she talks about her healing work. She knows this is her path, and yet, is unsure of how to make it all work. We aren't always ready to address each and every issue in our lives. When we feel enough pain and suffering from what doesn't work anymore, the impetus to change becomes greater and greater. Sometimes that's hard to see. Pausing will help us see more clearly.

A few months after our initial 10-week program completed, Bonnie called me feeling pretty stressed. She said, "I have overcommitted myself. I can't seem to follow through with anything, and my husband and my daughter are really suffering because of it. I've lost track of my priorities. The office is offering a business coach to help with time management, but I know I would get so much more than that from you." I beamed, and we began another 10-week program.

Her desire was to become a proficient time manager. She wanted to be more efficient, but didn't want her family and her spirituality to suffer because of it. She identified her priorities as family and relationships, spirituality, and finances. With the mortgage business revitalized, she set a goal to make six figures. However, the chaos and stress got so high that she lost touch with her juiciness and no longer knew what she wanted. She felt overwhelmed, angry, unhappy, dried up, stressed out, and had a terrible tightness in her chest. The practice of PAUSE is so simple, and yet so elusive.

At the beginning of all of my sessions, there is a short pause or meditation that I lead. As for Bonnie, this is one of the most valuable aspects of our work. Once she felt all the underlying feelings within her body, it didn't feel great. Each week she got closer to getting her priorities in line with her values and life. She had a "breakdown" in the process. That can happen when we lose complete sight of the bigger picture. Our sessions together were a time for her to collect her thoughts, pause and get clarity.

One of the things my clients can always count on me for is that I will remind them of their juiciness. I will remind them of the beautiful and luscious female that they are. As Bonnie began to lean into her juiciness, she began to crave a more satisfying adventure in play. She began to allow the good, tingly warm, happy energy that came with tuning back into her sexuality. She then felt moments of relief as she became aware of her unrealistic expectations.

She was still working too hard, and finally acknowledged that there was just too much day-by-day chaos. Bonnie is a beautiful and juicy woman who is a fabulous mom. I encouraged her to step into the new feminine leader that she is, and live through embracing her beauty and sexuality. I also encouraged her to imagine me sitting on her shoulder saying, "PAUSE and breathe."

Client Sandra

Sandra is working in the corporate healthcare industry and also has a private practice of energy work out of her home. She is 46 years old. Sandra had chronic issues of candida that made sex painful. Most of the time she felt comfortable with her beauty and the aging process, but she had her down times too. She felt the most comfortable focusing on her eyes, even though she worked out regularly and was extremely fit. She married a very athletic and successful businessman she met in her teens, and their marriage ended in divorce about 20 years later. She is currently in a solid relationship with a colleague. She has a sexual trauma history and feels tense and guarded in her second and third chakras.

Her boyfriend moved in, which was "great and stressful." She had been on her own for five years without answering to anyone. He was a real anchor for her. He encouraged her to slow down and feel more relaxed and peaceful with her life. He didn't do much outside of work, while Sandra had a very busy social life. She suffered from tightness in her belly, with her schedule being part of the cause.

Sandra's work with me centered on acute observation of her energy. Because she was such an empath, it was easy for people to suck her energy. Families can be some of the worst vampires. She was so energy-sensitive and always sounded tired on our calls. As we wrapped up our sessions, the new awarenesses for Sandra were to clear out the bad history, bring her inner child into her heart, and protect her energy system by setting shields on a daily basis. Her enjoyment of her sexuality and beauty are very tied into her health issue.

As is so common with chronic issues (don't I know it), she can feel despair and fear, which of course exacerbates the issue. Her strategy to take sensuality breaks with a 100 percent presence to the sights, sounds, smells, tastes and touches is where our work ended, for now. She turned some corners knowing that she is ready and willing to look inside and show up for herself in new ways. She is learning how to receive love from herself.

Client Maryanne

Maryanne is a lawyer and a chef, 50 years old. She feels darn good about her life. She has good genes, feels fit, has good skin, and lives life upbeat. She is married and a mom of four boys. Her sexuality was awakened at 40 when she had an extramarital affair. She became angry at her husband during this time because their sex was unfulfilling and filed for divorce. She retracted that decision for the sake of the family, but continued to cultivate other lovers.

Her vision of sexual liberation is living a life free from the parents and the Catholic Church, and making decisions based on what makes her feel good. She felt guilt about her extramarital affairs as her husband did not know, and she felt it would be disastrous for the family. Her first assignment was to repeat the affirmation, "I am at peace with my sexuality."

She was a quick study and embraced her sexuality by exploring the perspective of pleasure for pleasure's sake. Her openness and willingness to PAUSE and try on new thinking allowed her to integrate the changes very quickly. An inner peace began to replace the questions of guilt and remorse that she used to feel. With each PAUSE, she began to tap into the juicy energy and quickly embraced the power of it. The next week she showed up having slept well, feeling rested and happy.

She brought her juicy energy to having fun with her children. Her connection with her children and her husband grew stronger as she worked on inner peace. Her friends reflected back to her their perception of what a powerful and strong woman she was, and she received the feedback. She experienced feelings of courage, confidence and grace while embracing new liberation and freedom. It was not lost on her husband either. She burst through a barrier and responded to her husband's touch for the first time in many years.

Maryanne embraced the coaching work with 100 percent presence, focus and commitment. Being the high achiever she is, she absorbed the new concepts and valued the wisdom of our work. When asked how her 10-week coaching experience went, she responded with, "It wasn't just life-changing, it was life-altering."

No matter what your age or circumstance, you can awaken your beauty and sexuality. It is never too late to enliven your spirit with peace, passion, and pleasure.

Up next, we'll capture a final inspiration about PAUSE in this section before we move onto PONDER and PULSE in sections 2 and 3.

Chapter 8

Moving to Pleasure

We have beauty and sexuality all around us from which we can derive sensuality and pleasure. Does that surprise you? Try this ... PAUSE and think of the most beautiful person you know. What characteristics make you feel their beauty?

When you consider this question, it will bring you more into your pleasure center ... just by thinking about it. And when you lean into that pleasure center, you can experience the juicy feelings of your inner sexuality. I know, I know ... it sounds too simple, and there is more to awaken you in the next two books in the series on PONDER and PULSE. For now, you can move to more pleasure by integrating PAUSE into your life. That plants the seeds for the next two pieces of the pie AND for living what I call an organic and orgasmic life.

Living an Organic and Orgasmic Life means embracing all of your experiences and squeezing the juice out of them. It means not judging yourself or others as good, bad or otherwise. It means that every moment has some aliveness for you. This is a very healthy place to live. It's good for your overall well-being as well as your immune and cardiovascular systems. We know our orgasmic nature through sex; however, sex is not required for you to feel alive and juicy in your body.

Using our sexuality as medicine is not a common prescription, because you don't need to see a doctor for this kind of treatment. Why don't we use it more often? Why don't we share this information openly? It is common knowledge that we suppress sexuality in our world, especially in certain countries like the U.S. These antiquated ideas create much more backlash and unhealthy sex. The suppression expresses itself as extramarital affairs, and can even create illness. This is such a crime, given what we know about its healing powers.

What underlies the suppression is dishonesty. We are dishonest with our own sexual fulfillment and aliveness, and then we bring that dishonesty to our relationships. Faking orgasms instead of speaking the truth to our partners is one example. It is a vicious cycle of unhappiness that is not necessary if we PAUSE and tell ourselves the truth. Have you experienced healing through sexual pleasure?

How can you know whether or not your sexual relationship is healing?

1) Be honest with your pleasure meter during sex.

2) Does the pleasure last beyond the act of sex?

3) Can you recreate the feelings you experience during sex? These are some areas to PONDER. This gives you a brief preview of how "Healing with Pleasure: PONDER" will help. You know you are experiencing sexual healing when you experience the sensations and feelings of the pleasure long after the sex is over. This is a sign that you are accessing your inner sexuality. Your inner sexuality can help you ground your emotions and ignite your creativity. In your energy system, the emotions, creativity and sexuality are all located together in the second chakra area behind your belly button. See if you can feel it there.

The system, "The 3 Ps to Peace, Passion and Pleasure," is designed for women to uncover their inner beauty as well as their inner sexuality. This kind of beauty is lasting and true no matter what kind of hair day you may be having or how old you feel. This is important because women are disconnected to feeling good on the inside.

We have evidence of it everywhere with 10,000 women in the U.S. having eating disorders, expensive plastic surgeries, and the fast-growing market of anti-aging products and services. Doesn't it seem odd that it is inevitable to get older, and yet we fight it as if it is a horrible fate? This is especially true for women, and it's because they are disconnected with their inner beauty. So when the skin ages and wrinkles set in, many women feel old and used up. The disconnection is not only for older women though. Unfortunately, it is most women. Ninety-seven percent of women do not like something about their bodies.

This is a definite WHOA Baby worth a PAUSE. The reasons behind the difficulties that women have in their ability to stop and focus on their own self-care have been, in part, revealed through the brain science of the last two decades. Prior to the 1990s, all the studies in medicine were done on the male brain, because a woman's hormones would "screw up the data." Even studies on the pill were based on the male brain ... now there is a scary thought!

The corpus callosum is the connector between the brain's left and right hemispheres. In a woman's brain, it is wider, which makes it easier for her to take the kids to school, plan dinner tonight, prepare for the business meeting, and do her Kegel exercises on the way. Can you just feel how the brain is dancing around, keeping her up in her head instead of in her body? It does not take a rocket scientist to know that peace, passion and pleasure are felt in the body ... not thought about in the head. You cannot think your way to peace, passion and pleasure.

This movement toward more feminine energy and power in the world is happening. Let's make sure it is a peaceful and loving feminine energy. The only way for that to happen is for women to learn to love themselves again and feel their beautiful souls.

What's Next?

In Part 2 in this three-part series, we will explore our perspectives, thoughts, emotions, and feelings so we know how to change our views when they don't support our path. I'll share studies on positivity and how to integrate it into your life. Sensuality, self-love examples, along with a model for how to find the 100 percent pure energy of YOU are just a few peeks at Part 2. Pleasure Medicine is just inside waiting for you!

Part 2

PONDER

Chapter 1

What does it really mean to PONDER?

Let's dig deeper into what I mean by pondering to feel more peace, passion and pleasure. After you gain momentum toward mastering PAUSE, you will be able to direct and guide your thinking, being and feeling with powerful pondering questions and continue to access information about yourself.

This process is never over unless we call it quits. Our inner world is what we have the most control over in our lives, so it is beneficial to know how to satisfy and fulfill yourself on the inside. I am talking about understanding what makes you feel good, happy, sexual and beautiful from within. Can you imagine how grounded, centered and balanced you would feel if you could master the PONDER? When you do, interacting with the outside world flows with ease.

Let me dissect different approaches to PONDERing. There are many approaches to this word. What is in common with most, if not all, is that they involve active focus. Here are three approaches to PONDERing which demonstrate the benefits of understanding and shifting your experience.

The first approach to pondering is to contemplate what is going on right now in your life. For example, explore the pondering questions of: "What gives me energy? What takes my energy? Who gives me energy? Who zaps my energy?" These questions are asking you to get an overview of what is happening in your life's energy. Often, eliminating energy-draining people and situations or adopting new perspectives can dramatically shift your experience into something more positive and replenishing.

PONDERing from my second approach is to sit with and cogitate on a new perspective or idea. Maybe it's an idea that you never imagined yourself considering. Those are moments when you know you are expanding and pushing out from the edges of your comfort zone. You might PONDER what your life would look like if you thought another way. This approach often comes when someone plants a seed, a wild thought, that for some reason is creating excitement within you. The slowing down of PAUSE and PONDER is key to noticing the results of new perspectives. I used to put PONDER this (fill in the blank) on my to-do list. I then began to realize that to PONDER a new way of thinking involves becoming that new way of thinking.

In the final approach about pondering, we will explore what happens when we "lean in" to our feelings. Turn up the volume on your feelings, whether it's happy or sad. Creating the intention for "leaning in" is all about understanding who you are and getting clarity on what you want. When you know who you are and what you want, there is so much less confusion in life. Keep in mind you are ever-evolving and learning. This is not a static place we live. It's kind of like you get an aha, and then the doors start flying open to explore. I do hope you value adventure!

As we examine the first approach, take a closer look at identifying what is happening in your life right now. This will give you quick overview, or meta-view, of what's working and what's not. This is good information. Whether you choose to change anything at this point or not, at least there is a deeper understanding of what's going on beneath the surface. When we allow ourselves to PAUSE and PONDER, our bodies will undoubtedly share some wisdom with us. And the more we practice pausing and pondering and listening to the wisdom of our bodies, the more we know how to take care of and nourish ourselves. Relying more on the inside and less on the outside is a place of new freedom from the chaotic world.

When I initially came off of all of the pharmaceutical medication that I had been taking for 15 years, I began to feel the people and places in my life in a very different way. This was a situation where I had no choice but to pause, and when I did I decided to ponder the questions of who and what gives me energy and who and what takes my energy. I was met with answers that surprised me.

One result of that exploration was my need to disengage with a friend of mine who had been in my life for about 10 years. Along with our personal relationship, our children were friends. She was always a challenging personality for me as she was never on time, constantly had too much on her plate, and was difficult to get off the phone. While I was fatigued from my health, she would call. We would spend 20 minutes on the phone when I wished it was only a five-minute conversation because I was tired and didn't want to talk. After I finally got off the phone, I would roll over and fall asleep for an hour and a half. It became obvious to me that something in my relationship with this woman needed to shift.

It wasn't easy. She didn't want to change anything, and yet for a number of years I kept strong boundaries by not seeing her socially or talking with her on the phone. I explained myself as best as I could through both email and short phone calls, and then I would let go. The decision empowered me and helped me discern in a closer way the energies of other people. I began to set better boundaries, which did a world of good for my health and my life.

Special note about the word Ponder:

When you hear the word ponder, do you go to your head or do you go to your body? Both of these places have valuable wisdom for you. If you always go to your head to think about a question, next time go to your body first. When I say go to your body, I mean notice where there is tension, where there is relaxation and calm, where there is tightness and pain, and any and all sensations you become aware of. The wisdom is in your body.

Now let's look at the second approach on PONDERing, which is to adopt a different perspective or thought, and "try it on" for a week or two. Notice what happens. This takes commitment and awareness, and I promise you it is worth the effort. I love to plant seeds of possibility for people. For thousands of years we have been learning primarily by listening to others. It is now time to learn with guides on the outside but focus on the inside. What turns you on? What unique way do you feel beautiful and sexual? How sensual is your life?

One of the myths I love to bust and have my female clients ponder is that women dry up sexually as they age. This is in ancient myth that has been carried through the ages, and it is so destructive for our world. Aging women that are in touch with their sexuality, beauty and sensuality vibrate wise and juicy energy to the planet. I, for one, can state the false nature of the claim that we dry up. What if you believed that you get juicier as you age?

Wait a minute, you mean changing the way I think about something can actually change the energy I experience from a person or situation? Yes, that is exactly what I'm saying. Let me give you an example. I had a client who had a government job, and her boss was, to put it mildly, a very large pain in the neck. He constantly nitpicked on her work. She said at one of our sessions, "It is almost like he is preying on me."

She had worked there for over 10 years and had so much retirement and status built up that she did not want to have to start over again. However, she was caught in the same old cycle and trap that she had been in for the last 10 years. This woman had been referred to me because she had chronic fatigue and chronic pain, and she believed the stress of the work situation created it. She was adamant about not leaving, so we looked at how she could "try on" a new perspective around working with her boss.

It was time to stretch her to consider something out of the box.

I asked her, if he is preying on you, then what kind of animal are you? I asked her to visualize both she and her boss as animals that reflect how it feels to be preyed upon. Then I asked her what kind of animal she wanted to be. What does that look like in the work setting? The next week she showed up and said she is going to be and act like the honey badger at work. The honey badger is famous for its fearlessness and tenacity to go for what they want no matter what the obstacles. If it doesn't work the first time, the honey badger gets up and keeps going.

My client embraced the persona of the honey badger at work and became tenacious about fairness and honesty. She even went so far as to order a stuffed honey badger to keep on her desk to remind her of her intention. Eventually, her co-workers joined in the fun. Humor is an awesome way to lighten an energy-draining situation. When we PONDER a new perspective, it opens the door to humor and creative problem solving.

The third and final approach we will discuss here is "leaning in" to various situations and allowing our bodies to guide us. Last night, my roommate and I went to see the movie "Miss Representation," written and directed by Jennifer Siebel Newsom. Newsom documented the role of the media in how women and young girls feel about themselves.

You can imagine that some of the information was horrifying, such as, "People learn more from media than any other source of information," and "American teenagers spend 10 hours and 45 minutes a day watching media." My roommate left the showing angry. As she leaned into her anger, it brought up a realization that she felt bullied by the male establishment. Although it didn't feel good to viscerally experience the anger, it led her to stand up for herself and feel her power. The "come from" is not about putting men down. It's about women standing tall, knowing they have a voice that is needed.

Another example of the media's powerful influence is Liz Canner's movie, "Orgasm Inc." The movie highlights how we fall prey to advertising from pharmaceutical companies that create diagnoses of illnesses such as "female sexual dysfunction." That alone is pretty scary, but the movie continues to disturb with interviews where Canner asks the CEO of a major pharm company, "Where did this female sexual dysfunction diagnosis come from?" He sat PONDERing before saying, "I just don't know." What do you think? Is it real or made up by the company to create a drug to treat it?

On the radio recently, I heard an advertisement for "shift disorder syndrome." The medication was designed to help those working the night shift, because it isn't natural to sleep during the day and be awake at night. So let's get this straight, they want us to take medication because we are going against nature. Does that make sense to you?

What insights do you have when you "lean in" to your feelings around these situations? We must begin to live our lives standing up for what is right and eliminating the insanity. I'm not suggesting you lean into the fright and horror of every story on the news.

Learn and lean in to what you care deeply about. Lean in and stimulate the passion that supports what you know is right and true. Then take some action.

I have one more seed for you to PONDER: Dr. Vandana Shiva's work around the native seed, the beginning of how we grew food. I had the honor and pleasure to interview her at Dominican University in San Rafael, California, in 2011. She has a passionate message focusing on banning all chemical fertilizers and returning to organic gardening with the native seed. She lectures and inspires all over the world that the native seed is going through a holocaust as corporations are controlling seed supply.

Over 250,000 Indian farmers have committed suicide because of large indebtedness to these corporations. Dr. Shiva urged women to take back control of food for the future of our planet. Dr. Shiva was named one of the most seven most influential women in the world by Forbes magazine. Ever the optimist, Dr. Shiva began her talk with, "There is so much to celebrate, but we are in a mess."

I could write an entire book on approaches to PONDERing. There are so many valuable aspects to PONDERing, questions from "What did you love about your life in childhood?" to "How productive is chaos?" Powerful questions open you up to expanded inner thoughts that are stepping stones to a deeper knowing.

Rx from Chapter 1

1) Take 15 minutes in the next two days to journal the answer to these two questions.

    - What gives you energy?
    - Who gives you energy?

2) Plan to increase the time you spend with the what and who of your answers.

Now let's take a deeper look (PONDER) at how being 100 percent YOU affects your life.

Chapter 2

Your 100 Percent Pure Energy

In this remarkable journey of life, we are confronted with choices at every bend and turn. What helps guide your choices? What is the difference between a good choice and a bad choice? Experience has shown me that when I make a good choice, it originated in my intuition. Choices that hold some regret for me are when I have let outside forces override my inner truth. I inevitably feel badly when my core values have been compromised, and I have no one to blame but myself.

When you are making decisions from your intuition, you are moving with the rhythm of your own pure energy. Let me explain how I get to feeling my 100 percent energy place.

There was a time in early 2000 that I wanted to understand my energy and the energetic part of having a chronic pain condition. I enrolled in classes at the Academy of Intuition Medicine in Sausalito, California. It was there that I learned about grounding, chakras and auras.

When I need to ground myself in my own truth, this is the way that I do it.

1. I stop whatever I'm doing

2. I close my eyes

3. I take a nice, deep breath down into my lower belly

4. I imagine my energy moving down the back of my spine on the exhale. Extending from the base of my spine is a cord that pierces the earth and travels through all its different layers, wrapping around the core. I take another breath and feel the surface beneath me. Ahhh ... mother earth is always there supporting me.

5. I open my feet chakras and bring the dark green earth energy through my feet, cleansing all seven chakras with this marvelous energy.

6. It is important to set your chakras, and just below I will describe how to do that. This is only a guide.

7. Once your grounding cord is in place and your chakras are set, now it is time to create intention around your auric space.

8. Imagine a bubble surrounding your body, about five feet all around your body and underneath your feet. Within this space is pure 100 percent you.

These are the eight steps I use to set my energy space. You may be asking how you do it. How do you open your feet chakras or create a grounding cord? Your scientific mind might not understand, but you do it by intention. Feel the mysterious power of it. Don't question too much.

What you have to look forward to in book No. 3 in this series, "PULSE," is understanding how to vibrate your 100 percent pure energy out into the world.

"You are unique. If that is not fulfilled, something is lost."

– Martha Graham

I am such an advocate for nourishing and strengthening our inner world, as it is a key to happiness, peace and joy. Let me share a helpful way to understand your inner world. We'll break it down so you can see the numerous ways you can develop your ability to make decisions that will honor you and your values. That is what I call BEing 100 percent YOU. This does not mean that we take the attitude of, "It's my way or the highway." However, compromise is never wise when it means you have to set your values aside to accommodate someone else's desire or need. The reverse is also true. It is always wise to honor your values when you compromise.

You may have heard of the Wheel of Life, which illustrates how to examine 8-10 different aspects of your life and rate your satisfaction in each area. This is a beautiful snapshot of your life in the moment and how much it is flowing or not flowing. Below is the Wheel of Life I have used with hundreds of clients. They absolutely love it, because there is so much information for them in scoring their wheel. Not only do they see what's not working (where most clients want to focus), but it shows them in a very visual way the parts of their life that have great fulfillment and satisfaction. Most people have some good going on in at least one wedge of the wheel.

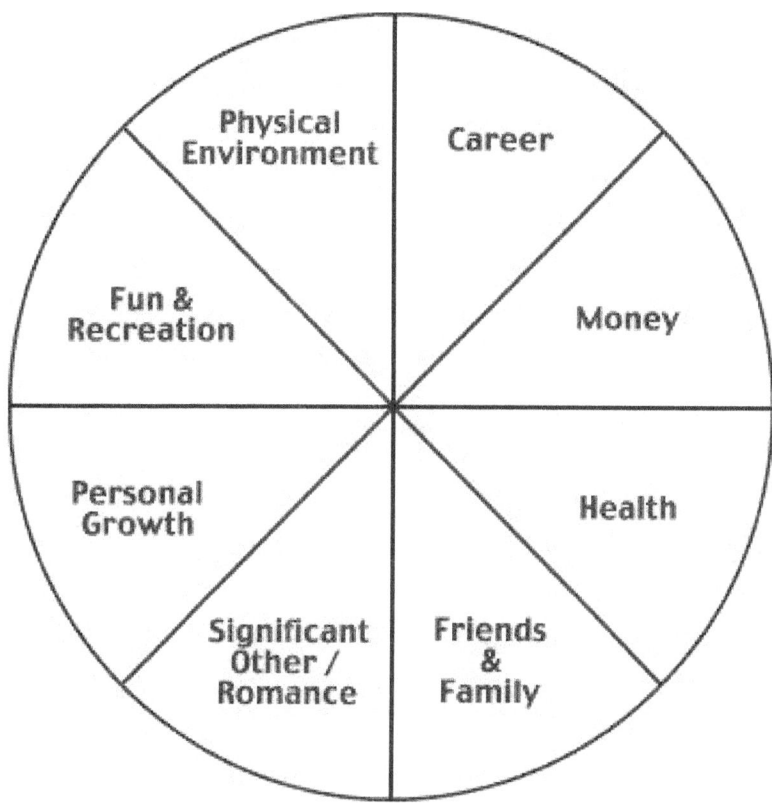

I have taken this same concept and designed eight aspects of your inner world. There are more, but this is demonstrates how dissecting down can create more avenues for simple, easy changes to enhance your state of well-being and generate good feelings about yourself. Evaluating the wheel will also reinforce your values and what it means to be in your 100 percent pure energy.

My mission is to help people rediscover their inner beauty, sensuality and sexuality so they fall in love with themselves every time they look in the mirror. Inner Beauty, Inner Sensuality, and Inner Sexuality are three aspects of your inner world. Cultivating your inner juiciness has an impact on the other five aspects of peace, truth, happiness, strength and love. It's true, when you nurture one, you feed all of them.

Below are simple ways to feed each one of these eight aspects. You may also want to declare your satisfaction for each aspect by choosing a number from 1 (not at all satisfied) to 10 (could not feel more fulfilled). Then practice the simple exercises and repeat, rating your satisfaction in a week. See if anything has changed.

Beauty: When you look in the mirror, look past the blemishes into your eyes. Say, as you are staring into those soulful eyes, "I love you. I really, really do." The "really, really do" part is very important. The more you practice, the deeper you go.

Sexuality: Place your hand on your lower belly (in between your pubic bone and belly button) and envision a fountain of healing power living right underneath your hand. Practice and cultivate this feeling during sex or anytime you feel like it. It's all right there.

Sensuality: Become more sensual. Feel the weather on your skin. Is it warm, wet, cold, windy? Just feel it. Sensuality brings you into the moment. This is something you can practice anytime or anywhere. It is only a shift of your attention. It brings more aliveness to ordinary situations.

Peace: Pause, Breathe and remember there is not another soul on the planet like you. Therefore, you will never really fit in and that is a good thing. Describe your body sensations when you identify a feeling of peace, and be specific. If you don't believe you ever feel or have felt peace on the inside, commit to a practice of PAUSE and Breathe at least 10 times a day.

Truth: The most reliable truth you have is to listen to your body. What signal is your body giving you about your inner world? When you are lined up with your truth, your body is calm and relaxed. The opposite is also true. When you are out of alignment with your values, your body is tense and stressed. Notice what is present when your body is calm and relaxed. Write it down in your journal.

Happiness: Laughter is the quickest way to happiness. Finding joy and fun comes easy for some; however, those who have a big drive for accomplishment or have a serious and intense personality may have a harder time finding the funny. Laughing is an immediate stress release, and laughter yoga shows us that you don't even have to be in the mood to laugh for it to work. Watch a funny movie, read jokes or contact someone you know who brings light and laughs to conversation. Norman Cousins healed himself from crippling arthritis through the medicine of laughter.

Strength: REMOVE victim mentality from your language and thoughts. There is no one to blame for how things are working for you. Identify where you feel strong in your life. Repeat it out loud to yourself, write about it in your journal, and create reminder notes in your home, car and work space to remind you often of your strength. Pay attention to it and build on the feeling!

Love: Hug yourself every morning before you get out of bed, even if you have someone else to hug you. The more you fall in love with yourself, the more you will know you deserve pleasure.

You can see there are many ways to nourish and love yourself up. This is the pathway to knowing that living in 100 percent of your pure energy is what feels the best to you and what serves the world the best, too.

The more you cultivate your inner world, the more you will be able to relate to anyone, anytime and anywhere with courage, confidence and grace.

Rx from Chapter 2

1) Choose at least one of the Inner World Wheel of Life aspects and commit to one simple practice each day for the next week. It will enhance and nourish that wheel aspect.
2) Practice the eight steps to ground, and set your aura. Do it every day for at least three weeks. Notice and journal about the difference you feel, if anything.

Another amazing way to shift your energy and raise your vibration is to tap into positivity and optimism as a way of life. The next chapter has some compelling evidence as to why it is a wonderful stress reliever.

Chapter 3

Positive Optimism for Well-Being

I couldn't wait to write this chapter. This is one of my favorite topics, and I have so much to share with you on exploring ways that we can hold the attitude and perspective of optimism. There is some pretty interesting scientific evidence for the power of positive emotions presented by University of California researcher Dr. Judy Moskowitz, along with three very powerful women and their stories of optimism and positivity. Open up to your spirit being lifted as you read through the gems of this chapter!

For starters, the list below contains 10 ways to keep grounded in positivity. These are simple practices that keep your body functioning at an optimal level. And when we are functioning at an optimal level, we have more brain power and energy to see and experience things as hopeful and happy.

1) Breathe deeply. Make a commitment to breathe for 30 seconds deep down into your belly when you arise every morning.

2) Joke. Find your funny. Have a few jokes handy to create some healthy and healing laughter. Laugh at yourself often.

3) Smile at anyone and everyone, including yourself in the mirror.

4) Sleep. Write down how many hours of sleep you have on your calendar in the morning. Each week note your average. Try to go for an average of eight hours a night.

5) Eat something healthy that you enjoy every day. Maybe it's just a banana in the morning. Note how good it feels to eat it.

6) Drink at least one liter of hot water every day. First thing in the morning is ideal. This is not boiling, but as hot as you can drink it. Add lemon for some added flavor and health benefits.

7) Meditate every morning for at least five minutes. Nothing fancy needed, you can basically sit quietly with yourself.

8) Dance to your favorite music for five minutes a day. Choose a song that makes you let loose a little.

9) Take at least 10 deep breaths out in the fresh air. This could be on the way to the car or on the way into the shopping center. Just notice the air.

10) Look at your body in the mirror every day after you shower or bathe. Let it know that you are paying attention.

These 10 ideas are pretty basic, and yet can make a huge difference if you implement them with self-love. No judgment is acceptable when we are developing new healthy habits.

Let me share this quote with you from a book called "Positivity," by Dr. Barbara Fredrickson. "Positive emotions in a 3 to 1 ratio with negative ones lead people to a tipping point beyond where they naturally become more resilient to adversity and effortlessly achieve what once they could only imagine. And 80 percent of Americans fall short of the 3 to 1 ratio."

That's an awful lot of negativity. Do we need to be convinced of the value of the positive optimism?

Let me see if I can convince you!

Dr. Judy Moskowitz, Professor of Medicine at the University of California-San Francisco, has been studying how positive emotions help you cope with stress. When we have skills to deal with stress, we have less pain and greater health. Her research about positive thinking and emotions is based on her work with HIV-positive AIDS patients and their partners in the 1990s when their diagnosis was considered fatal.

I interviewed Judy in 2009 because I heard her speak about a National Institutes of Health (NIH) bereavement longitudinal study on how stress and coping skills affect the body both physically and psychologically. The group they chose to study was men caring for their partners with AIDS. They interviewed these caregivers who were undergoing some of the most horrible stress a human can experience. While the caregivers were absolutely stressed and upset, as you would expect, they also had positive things going on that they wanted to tell the researchers about.

When I asked Judy who it was that thought to look at these positive emotions, she told me it was the participants that queued the health care professionals about positive emotions playing a role in relieving stress. In the mid-1990s, this was not yet looked at by psychology. NIH went along with the idea to study correlations between positive emotions and stress. What they found was that people with positive emotions live longer. Also noted was that people with positive emotions who have chronic pain take better care of themselves. Judy and her colleagues are now working to help health care professionals recognize the important role of positive emotions in health. Judy shared that if providers deal better with their own stress, then they are able to provide more help for their patients.

Judy and her team developed 10 positive emotions skills. Here are three samples:

1) Notice positive events. Good things happen all the time and all you have to do it notice.

2) Capitalize on those good things. When something good happens, tell someone and write about it so you can re-experience the positive emotion. The flipside of that is also true; when we ruminate on bad things, we re-live the negative emotions.

3) Engage in acts of kindness. Stress will often keep us self-focused and ruminating on our situation. When we do nice things for others, we live

longer, healthier lives. In one very cool study Judy shared with me, they took 20 people and gave them $20 and told them to go spend it on themselves. Then they took 20 more people and gave them $20 and told them to go spend it on someone else. When all of the participants were called later that evening, the results showed that those that had spent the money on someone else were much happier.

Now I want to tell you about three powerful women that used positivity, optimism and skipping (yes, skipping!) as a way to contribute good stuff to the world.

The perfect person to start with is Ms. Valeri Bocage. Valeri is the founder of Powerful Women International and has been assisting people with living their dreams for over 20 years. She has inspired hundreds of people to fulfill their life's mission. She has coached authors, entrepreneurs, parents, families, public speakers and artists to expand their vision globally for what was possible in their professional and personal lives. She has been recognized by the United States Congress, U.S. Senate, mayoral offices, and several companies and organizations around the world.

Valeri was born and raised in New Orleans, Louisiana. As a result of Hurricane Katrina, she lost everything, except her indomitable spirit and true passion for life. When I asked her what it was like to experience Katrina, she said, "I always try to do my best to look at the bright side and make the best of things." She wasn't in New Orleans at the time. She had been transferred to Florida, where she described watching TV and seeing her city "go down." She was wondering where her daughter was. It was traumatizing. She said to herself, "How am I going to make the best of this?"

She located her daughter several days later and asked, "Okay God, now what? When I pray, I get really quiet so I can listen to the inner voice. It said, 'It's time to fulfill your purpose'". That's when she moved to San Francisco and started holding events with women to share their victory stories. The premise for the whole organization is to celebrate victories and success – the ultimate example of positive optimism. From that first meeting in San Francisco, Powerful Women International has grown globally, with more cities coming on all the time.

Some of Valeri's ideas about how to have a positive outlook include: "I do my best to surround myself with good happy thinking people; I'm not religious but I pray a lot, and I know that worrying zaps my creativity and my energy." Carry on, Powerful Valeri!

My next radio guest you get to learn about is the upbeat and fun Kim "Skipper" Corbin. Kim started skipping for fun and fitness over 10 years ago. It turned into much more than that. It became a way to help shift the world to a more positive place.

Kim has been the world's most vocal advocate for the body, mind and spirit benefits of adult skipping since she created the iskip.com website in 1999. Her efforts have been featured in USA Today, Time, People and Newsweek magazines.

Kim's vision of a skipping movement was an inspiration that came from within. In 1999, she became committed to her own fitness, started skipping, and found that it was good for her body, mind and spirit. She says she can't help but be happy while she's skipping. Her brother helped her start the website and she began holding skipping events in San Francisco.

The *San Francisco Chronicle* did an article about her, and at the next event 80 people showed up. Such a turnout brought Kim and her skipping national media attention. For her, the idea behind the skipping movement is about freedom and fun. But the fitness community took skipping very seriously and focused on the many fitness benefits of skipping. For instance, it burns twice as many calories as walking and has half of the impact on your joints as running.

The other gem of a point that Kim made on the interview is that we are always so worried in our culture of what other people think of us. She saw skipping as a help to strengthen the muscle of her own spirit of joy and bliss, and she didn't worry about what other people thought. When asked what kinds of responses she got when she skipped down the streets of San Francisco, she said overall her experience is receiving happiness in return.

Yvette Summers is the co-founder of Living an Organic and Orgasmic Life. She is a very special person who is one of the most positive people I have ever met. Her description of living an Organic and Orgasmic Life is finding a way to make every activity become love.

Yvette is a musicologist, percussionist, dancer and vocalist who has worked with Grammy Award-winning artists Herbie Hancock, Bill Summers and Los Hombres Calientes, to name a few. Her exotic and sensual dancing and singing will uplift your spirits and make you feel good. In 2010, we co-produced the "Living an Organic & Orgasmic Life" tour, a performance of music, dance and conversation that was musically rich and culturally diverse.

As we traveled together in Europe, we had many experiences where we got to practice taking mishaps and turning it into organic and orgasmic living. On the complete interviews in the Resource Section at the back, you can hear several stories from that trip that demonstrate how we integrated our work into our travels. It meant having faith and trusting that everything works out. And, it did. Yvette refers to it as "changing poison into medicine."

Yvette is unique in that she doesn't worry about money and has very little of her own. And yet, she has traveled the world and stayed in some of the most magnificent accommodations and eaten the most gourmet food available. Her gifts include smiling and bringing love to everyone she meets on her travels.

What is your relationship to positivity and optimism?

Rate yourself from 1 (not at all optimistic or positive) to 10 (live in optimism and positivity).

Rx from Chapter 3

1) What has been the most positive thing you have learned so far in this book on PONDER? How have you incorporated that learning into your life?

2) What are 10 positive events you have experienced in your life? What made them so?

PONDER these questions for at least a week, and then rate your positivity level again.

Let's take positivity to another whole level. In the next chapter, we will get into sensuality and self-love with none other than the "Queen of Self-Love," Christine Arylo.

Chapter 4

Sensuality and Self-Love

*"Self-love is the purest form of love.
It is you loving you so you can love the world more."*

- SARK (Susan Ariel Rainbow Kennedy)

When you are deeply in love with yourself, you are living a sensual life. When you are in alignment with your senses, you are showing yourself love. And so it goes that the two cannot be separated and enhance the quality of the other.

I am thrilled to share some experts of self-love with you. There cannot be enough emphasis on learning to love yourself, and yet there is no handbook for how to do it. This chapter will be the start of that handbook, as you hear from four different people from four distinct backgrounds sharing some how-to tips.

Susan Ariel Rainbow Kennedy, or SARK, as she is known in the literary community, has much to say about how juicy life becomes when we love ourselves. SARK is a best-selling author and artist, with 16 titles in print and well over 2 million books sold, including the national bestsellers "Succulent Wild Woman," "Bodacious Book of Succulence," "Eat Mangoes Naked," "Prosperity Pie," and "Juicy Pens, Thirsty Paper."

Her newest book is "Glad No Matter What." She is also the founder and Creative Fountain of Planet SARK, a thriving business that creates innovative products and services to support empowered living. SARK lives and creates gladly with her beloved partner John in San Francisco, California.

Here is some of SARK's brilliance:

"What's it like to live juicy where we make our most alive choices? Those choices that make the hair on the back of your neck stand up and you say, 'Oh. I don't know if I could do that.' It's about sexuality, but it's about everything, really. Sexuality is a reflection of how we live in every way. I have a really orgasmic life with myself. When I don't have a lover, I'm my own best lover. I have the most romantic dinners with myself, and even slow dance with myself."

"People are constantly taking the outside, like the weather, and having it change the way they feel on the inside. They say, 'If I just get this text message, or car, or new job, then I will feel good.' "

Imagine if that were always available to you because it came from the inside first?

There was a chance elevator encounter where SARK met a man who was smiling to himself, exuding so much wonderful energy that she had to mention it to him. He replied, "I am so in love with myself!" From that moment forward, she said, "Why am I not saying that? Why am I not living that?"

Coach Betty: "How do you fill your self-love cup?"

SARK: "I start each morning hugging myself before getting out of bed … at first it felt sort of ridiculous and I didn't feel the benefit. Now, I find myself taking 5-10 minutes of rolling around, kissing my shoulders, and saying terms of endearment. When I get out of bed, I feel like 12 good friends have hugged me, and all my endorphins have risen, and I feel like a full cup of self-love ready to share the overflow."

My next expert on self-love comes from the western medical community. What!? This is an inspiring example of what's possible when a doctor's heart is in the right place.

For many, Dr. Bernie Siegel needs no introduction. He has touched many lives all over the planet. In 1978, he reached a national and then international audience when he began talking about patient empowerment and the choice to live fully and die in peace. As a physician who has cared for and counseled innumerable people whose mortality has been threatened by illness, Bernie embraces a philosophy of living and dying that stands at the forefront of the medical ethics and spiritual issues our society grapples with today.

In May 2011, Bernie was honored by the Watkins Review of London as one of the Top 20 Spiritually Influential Living People on the planet. He continues to break new ground in the field of healing, supporting changes in medical education to "humanize" medical practice.

Bernie reaches out to women with the following message:

"What I want women to do is not live a role. Not to be Mama or the wife, and live an authentic life. So that they don't wait for a life threatening illness, and then say okay now I'm going to do what I want to do and not kill myself to make this marriage work." Bernie had to throw in a punch line from one of his cancer patients who said, "I got a mastectomy and a divorce. I gave up a tit and an ass."

"You've got to love your life and love your body. Then it gets the message that you want to stay alive and it does everything it can."

Bernie includes many miracle stories in his books. The one he told on-air was particularly moving. One of his patients shared, "My mother's words were eating away at me and maybe gave me cancer. She only dressed me in dark colors, and nobody would notice me. She told me I embarrassed her and was a failure." Now, this woman had cancer twice before her husband brought in one of Bernie's books. She told Bernie, "You gave me permission to be the person I was meant to be."

She needed permission, and I can attest that my clients give me the same feedback. Being given permission to feel your feelings is powerful. No blame on our parents, but parents' words are hypnotic up to the age of 6. Brain wave patterns in children prior to age 6 are similar to those that are under hypnosis. Bernie went on to say, "Our lives are stored in our organs." Read on to hear my own personal example of this.

A WHOA Baby statistic Bernie shared came from a Harvard study where students were asked if they were loved by their parents. After 35 years, individuals from the group that answered yes reported that only one out of four had a serious illness. In the group that answered no, 98 percent had serious health conditions. Being the special guy that Bernie is, he said he has learned to re-parent. One of his patients began calling him CD. He asked what that meant, and he said "Chosen Dad." Bernie suggests we all do that for each other to spread this love.

Remember, when you love yourself, everybody wins.

Now I want to share with you why I am so passionate about teaching self-love. As you know by now, much of my work has been inspired from my journey with Rheumatoid Arthritis (RA).

There are over 100 different forms of arthritis. Rheumatoid arthritis is characterized by painful, hot and swollen joints. It is considered an autoimmune disorder that affects the entire immune system and manifests in the body within the synovial fluid around the joints. Something in this fluid eats away at the tissues of the entire joint.

Medicine calls this an overactive immune system, which is why one of the ways you are treated for RA is with chemotherapy drugs (immune suppressants) to slow the progression of destruction in the joints. When the immune system is suppressed, your body is not attacking itself.

I began to take the immunosuppressant drug methotrexate about five years after being diagnosed. It was a difficult decision for me to take this medication as I had a 3-year-old daughter, Rebecca. Rebecca's dad and I were constantly fighting colds with the new preschool germs in the house. Methotrexate was the next level of serious drugs with potent side effects. This scared me. Was I really going to have to take these drugs for the rest of my life? These were some of the things I pondered in addition to a situation that made me very sad.

What I began to PONDER and came to understand about the physical manifestation of RA in my body was that it was a form of self-hatred. PAUSE on that for a moment.

I am not saying that this is true for everyone who has been diagnosed with rheumatoid arthritis. RA is one of those very unique conditions in that what works for one person may not work for another. When I first began to see rheumatoid arthritis as a form of self-hatred, it made a lot of sense to me.

As a people pleaser extraordinaire, I have abandoned myself more than once in the past. The most significant way this has shown up are the times I was dissuaded from pursuing the art of dance, which I adored my entire life. It happened when I was 6 and it happened again when I was 30. When I chose to step away from dance at 30 to please my husband, rheumatoid arthritis showed up in my body.

If you think about what Bernie Siegel says, that our lives are stored in our organs and our bodies, I believe anger had become stored in my joint tissue because I repeatedly stepped away from the essence of who I am, a dancer. This was not easy to see or feel, and yet I knew the deep truth of it.

Once I embraced the idea that it could be true that my rheumatoid arthritis meant I hated myself on some deep level, then I could begin the journey of self-love with amazing people like the "Queen of Self-Love," Christine Arylo.

Christine is a self-admitted, but recovering, achievement junkie and doing addict. She is an inspirational catalyst who writes and speaks about the struggles and possibilities this generation of woman — today's 21st century woman — faces in getting the love and happiness she works so hard to find.

The popular best-selling author of "Choosing ME before WE, Every Woman's Guide to Life," Christine is affectionately known as the Queen of Self-Love. This is a title she earned through her relentless commitment to teaching and inspiring people around the world to really, truly fall madly in love with themselves.

After leaving her six-figure corporate career behind, Christine spent the last decade dedicated to making self-love a tangible reality for all people. She is the creator of Madly in Love with ME™, an international self-love movement that includes an official self-love holiday on February 13 — put it on your calendar! She is the co-founder of Inner Mean Girl Reform School™, a virtual school and community that has helped over 25,000 women transform their self-sabotaging voices into self-loving ones.

Christine loves to speak, inspiring people to never settle for less than their heart and soul's desire. She has been a frequent guest on ABC, CBS, FOX and E! Entertainment TV, and she speaks often on college campuses, at retreat and spa resorts, and at conferences around the country. When not online teaching or on the mic talking, she is hanging out with her second-best friend – her partner Noah – because as Christine says, "Every person must choose to be their best friend first, knowing that when they choose the loving act for themselves, they ultimately take better care of those they love."

She started our interview with the current definition of self-love on dictionary.com, which includes harsh words such as conceit, vanity and narcissism. This definition is a reflection of how misunderstood self-love is within our culture. Christine asserts that most people know what they

SHOULD do to love themselves, but struggle to give themselves PERMISSION to take the self-loving act.

Christine recommends listening to her definition of self-love from your heart. She asks that you PAUSE, breathe deeply, and put your hand on your heart. "Self-love is the unconditional respect and love that you have for yourself that is so deep, so solid, so unwavering, that you only invite in and allow in that same respect and unconditional love."

She goes on to say, "We've become comfortable as a culture talking about self-esteem, but it isn't enough. Self-esteem is only one-tenth of self-love. And while it's great our kids are now getting the message they can do and be anything, children and adults alike feel pressured to do and be everything, which of course is impossible. So we fail, feel like we are not enough, and ultimately suffer – emotionally and physically.

The statistics on depression, unmarried pregnancies, drug use, stress-related disease, abusive relationships are not going down, and in many cases they are on the rise. We have to teach ourselves and our kids how to love themselves – not as a nice idea, but as a practical reality – and then making self-love as normal and acceptable as self-esteem."

Christine has a unique way of describing self-love that makes it so anyone can see what ways they do love themselves well, and which ways they need to grow their ability to choose love, "Self-love is like a tree. There are 10 branches including self-acceptance, self-esteem, self-care, self-empowerment, etc. — and a deep root system which is your self-worth. All 10 branches of self-love need to be strong and your self-worth roots need to be connected to internal value systems, not external measures."

Why is this so hard? One reason is that we set ourselves up to meet unrealistic expectations, which of course we always fall short on. Instead of giving ourselves A's in how well we are living our life, we judge ourselves harshly and give ourselves F's for things like:

Falling behind - "Everyone else is doing so much better than me."

Failing to measure up to the super woman standards - "I should be able to do more, achieve more, get more done."

Feeling like a fraud - "I don't really know what I am doing, and everyone is going to find out soon enough."

This internal voice is really the voice of the INNER Mean Girl -- that harsh, internal voice that sees what you are not doing. Christine is an expert at reforming this self-sabotaging voice for women through her virtual programs at Inner Mean Girl Reform School. She helps women transform their inner critics into their super heroine.

She went on to say that when we are not in love with ourselves, we are in fear. You may have heard of physical treatments such as a liver cleanse. Well, Christine has developed a 40-day inner fear cleanse, a practice that allows you to get close to what big, bad fears are driving you. We often do not have a clue what our fears are because we are told "don't be afraid." People have taken life-transforming steps when they look at their fears face-to-face.

PONDER the following love mantra that Christine says you can use in the moment when fear shows up, "I choose to release the fear, and I choose to have faith in love." Say it over and over again until the fear disappears. You will soon find that you are surrounded with people who love you unconditionally.

Since that interview, she has completed her second book, "Madly in Love with ME, the Daring Adventure to Becoming Your Own Best Friend."

My final guest interview to share in this chapter is Debra L. Reble, Ph.D, a Cleveland-based author, therapeutic intuitive and psychologist who conducts a private practice and facilitates workshops and seminars on personal transformation and well-being. She also is the founder of HeartPaths, a producer of materials inspiring full self-expression, and a director of

Foundation in Light, an international nonprofit educational organization furthering spiritual growth and self-realization.

In the provocative new model of relationship set forth in Soul-Hearted Partnership, Debra shows how dreams of amazing relationships come true when individuals cultivate first a soul partnership with themselves. Soul-Hearted Partnership lays the groundwork by presenting a series of spiritual principles for integrating body, heart, spirit and soul, and intertwining the combined energies with those of a loved one while acknowledging the shared energy source.

I asked Debra, "So we know that we want to love ourselves, but how do you do the work?"

The first step is becoming aware of yourself, your feelings. No matter what you feel, it is okay. Debra said we should get in touch with that and express the BEing (those feelings) that we are.

Once we become aware of our real feelings, the answers to why we get triggered become clearer. Trusting yourself and your feelings is understanding that you know what is best for you, even in the face of someone telling you, "Well, I wouldn't make that choice."

When you hit resistance within yourself, Debra helps her clients understand they have created the resistance to deal with an internal issue and should let go of the fear. She stressed that we need to take personal responsibility without being a victim.

Her soul-hearted partnership model is different, as she believes we have thousands of soul partners, maybe for a moment, a season, a reason, or a lifetime. The ones who last a lifetime are the soul-hearted partnerships. What is seen in these special partnerships is a commitment of self-exploration by both people, whether romantic, business or friends.

You approach another with your 100 percent pure, juicy energy as "I am whole and complete, and I offer that to you." That is a soul-hearted partnership.

A final piece I will share with you on sensuality and self-love is in the sexual arena. Sensuality is the foreplay to sexuality. Our beauty, sensuality, sexuality and self-love are some of the most natural things for us as human beings. And so I glean a quote from the magazine "Natural Solutions," "Multiple worldwide surveys show that 30 percent of women from teens to seniors report having little interest in sex."

This is a WHOA Baby to me because, as women, we ARE sexual BEings. When 30 percent of women have no interest in sex, then our women do not love themselves up overall. There are always special circumstances, however, when women are not connected with themselves and feeling good, then there are a whole lot of children, men and women unhappy. Remember that old saying, "When Mama ain't happy, nobody's happy!"

Here are my five secrets for women to manifest healthy, enjoyable, fun and replenishing sex.

1) Mellow out. Start with 30 seconds, three times a day to breathe and feel into your body (focus is on beauty, sensuality, sexuality and self-love).

2) Free yourself from outcomes and expectations. Let events unfold organically.

3) Live in the moment. Let your body feel the sensations of the moment.

4) Surrender to the pleasure. You do deserve it.

5) Thank your body for the experience. Don't miss this step!

Notice that these steps can be done with or without a partner. Love yourself up, and then others will automatically love you up, too.

Rx from Chapter 4

1) Write/Print Christine's definition and hang it in a prominent place in your world. Read it every day for 40 days (ooh, big challenge!!)

2) Redesign your relationship with yourself, including your body and pleasure. Practice the five steps to manifesting healthy, enjoyable, fun and replenishing sex.

Next up, we will have some fun with the leadership game "Fortunately/Unfortunately" and PONDER the Tao wisdom of "Who's to say what is good and what is bad?"

Chapter 5

Half-empty? Half-full?

Is the glass half-full or half-empty? From Bill Cosby's perspective, "It depends on whether you're pouring or drinking."

Mark Desvaux is quoted as saying, "Some people see the glass half-full, while others see the glass half-empty. The enlightened are simply grateful to have a glass."

And an anonymous brilliant comedian came up with, "It doesn't matter if the glass is half-empty or half-full, there is clearly room for more wine."

Now I've already written a whole chapter on optimism, so that's not what we're going to explore here. We're going to talk about the fact that there is a flip-side to everything. Actually, there are many flip-sides to everything, as we each are capable of holding hundreds of perspectives about the same thought or experience.

It is a fun experiment to ask a roomful of people how they view a common experience. If everyone tells the truth, you would get a unique view from each person of the very same experience. It points out how we are having a personal, individual experience in life. There is an internal conflict in most of us about wanting to belong to a group or community. Yet at the same time, we naturally want to be our unique, individual self and not get lost and swept up in the consensus of the group.

Another observation I have had of this phenomenon is with our political system. I have seen some Senate and House committee meetings broadcast on TV.

One such occasion was when Al Gore was presenting his findings and studies on climate change. Democrats and Republicans were represented on the committee and everyone received the exact same report. You probably see where I'm going with this. Yet the Democrats felt climate change was obvious from the statistics that were demonstrated by Gore, while the Republicans saw all the data as bunk. This is one reason why our political system is so ineffective.

It is far from ideal to quiet your own wants and needs for the good of the group, and it takes courage. It may even feel as though you are going against the flow if it is not your normal habit to stand your own ground.

So when you begin to PONDER the perspectives and attitudes that create what you want, the power of choice comes into play. Events happen and you do choose your thoughts. One of my coaching mentors used to say, "The thoughts in our heads and the words that come out of our mouths are the direction our lives will go in."

In the leadership program I attended and previously mentioned in book No. 1 on PAUSE, we played a flip side activity called "Fortunately/Unfortunately." Now the way this game worked was we sat in circles of about eight people, and somebody began a story with the word fortunately. Then the next person continued the story with unfortunately, and then the next person continued the story with fortunately. It continued around the circle in that way. The activity was such an eye-opener to see how there was always a fortunately and unfortunately point of view.

My group's story went something like this, "Fortunately, I know exactly what I want to have for dinner; unfortunately, I don't have all the ingredients I need; fortunately, there is a store close by that carries my ingredients; unfortunately, I'm not getting paid for a week and it will really stretch my budget; fortunately, I'm sharing dinner with my boyfriend so maybe he can kick in a little money…"

A deeper personal example might be, "Unfortunately, I have RA; fortunately, it is not life-threatening; unfortunately, there is pain and joint destruction which often accompanies it; fortunately, there are exercises I can do to maintain the functioning and range of motion; unfortunately, after so many years of inflammation, I have destruction and now need to get my hip replaced; fortunately, I am here in Arizona with excellent medical coverage where they do 10,000 hip replacements annually..."

Why bother with this silly little game? Because we really do get to choose whether we live in fortunately or unfortunately. In addition, if you talk the scenarios through at least a few fortunately/unfortunately(s), your energy will lift and your mood will lighten.

In SARK's book, "Glad No Matter What," she claims this book isn't like the annoying habit of when people try to tell you to feel glad when you don't feel glad. This book is about feeling your feelings and finding the glad within your feelings, and transforming and alchemizing the others. This is what SARK calls "practical gladness."

When you do this transformative practice, you get to live in the marvelous messy middle where you can embrace all your feelings at the same time. SARK went on to say, "The truth is we are many feelings at the same time. We can be glad and mad simultaneously. Those are not opposites, those are best friends." Can you wrap your mind around that one?

We are making choices, either conscious or unconscious, in response to everything that happens to us. Do you see yourself as a fortunately or unfortunately person?

Here is a twist on a fortunately/unfortunately situation:

A man wakes up in the hospital bandaged from head to foot.

The doctor comes in and says, "Ah, I'm glad to see you've regained consciousness. You probably won't remember, but you were in a huge pile-up on the freeway. You're going to be okay — you'll walk again and everything, but your penis was severed in the accident and we couldn't find it."

The man groans, but the doctor goes on. "You've got $9,000 in insurance compensation coming, and we now have the technology to build a new penis. They work great, but they don't come cheap. It's roughly $1,000 an inch." The man perks up.

"So," the doctor says, "you must decide how many inches you want. I understand that you've been married for over forty years and this is something you should discuss with your wife. If you had a nine-incher before and you decide to invest only in a five-incher now, she might be disappointed. It's important that she plays a role in helping you make a decision."

The man agrees to talk it over with his wife.

The doctor comes back the next day and asks, "So, have you spoken with your wife?"

"Yes, I have," says the man.

"And has she helped you make a decision?"

"Yes," says the man.

"What is your decision?" asks the doctor.

"We're getting granite countertops."

I'm not sure the fellow in the joke could take the Tao approach, but the story below illustrates why it is better to accept the wholeness of life instead of judging good and bad experiences.

When an old farmer's stallion wins a prize at a country show, his neighbor calls to congratulate him.

But the old farmer says, "Who knows what is good and what is bad?"

The next day some thieves come and steal his valuable animal. His neighbor comes to commiserate with him, but the old man replies, "Who knows what is good and what is bad?"

A few days later, the spirited stallion escapes from the thieves and joins a herd of wild mares leading them back to the farm. The neighbor calls to share the farmer's joy, but the farmer says, "Who knows what is good and what is bad?"

The following day, while trying to break in one of the wild mares, the farmer's son is thrown and fractures his leg. The neighbor calls to share the farmer's sorrow, but the old man's attitude remains the same as before.

The following week the army passes by, forcibly conscripting soldiers for a war, but they do not take the farmer's son because he cannot walk. The neighbor thinks to himself, "Who knows what is good and what is bad?" and realizes that the old farmer must be a Taoist sage.

- *From The Tao Book and Card Pack by Timothy Freke*

So I've told some stories and had some fun in this chapter; now let's break it down clean and simple.

The ABCs of Feeling

Action, Event or Circumstance: any situation you find yourself in, good or bad.

Beliefs and Self-Talk (can be half-empty or half-full): Your underlying beliefs and what you say to yourself.

Consequences or Results (can be positive or negative): The outcome you experience because of your beliefs and self-talk.

Since this book is about pleasure and healing, what beliefs and self-talk would make pleasure and healing more likely to be the result? PONDER that.

Rx from Chapter 5

1) Take an issue you are having in your life right this moment that feels challenging or a struggle. Start a fortunately/unfortunately story about it, and keep going until the energy and mood lighten.

2) Become acutely aware of your feelings throughout the day, taking cues from your body and breath. Identify the feeling words that go with the cues (fear, safe, mistrust, trustful, anger, secure, hurt, comfortable, upset, relaxed, etc.) PONDER how well you allow yourself to feel your feelings fully.

Now that you are more familiar with the flip sides of your story, let's look at why the story you tell yourself matters.

Chapter 6

The Story You Tell Yourself Matters

It was about the mid-1990s. My husband and I were in the chronic long haul with my rheumatoid arthritis. I was looking for some help for my relationship. I knew how hard this was on my husband because he couldn't fix it and I didn't know how to help him with that.

I learned of a new support group for people who had chronic pain conditions and their spouses, led by a psychotherapist. I thought to myself, maybe this will be good. Maybe it will be a place for us both to feel comfortable expressing how challenging this really is and get a few things off our chests.

We show up to the meeting in a large gym with folding chairs set in a circle. There were approximately three or four other couples who came to check it out. The psychotherapist stood up and began the meeting with the following question, "Who is the IP?" We all looked at her a bit confused. Then she clarified, "IP stands for ill person." When I heard her say that, my blood began to boil. IP? Who on earth would ever want to be considered an IP? I had to speak up. I said, "Don't call me in IP! I am a healthy person with rheumatoid arthritis."

Even as I write this now, I can still feel the energy that I felt in the gym that evening so long ago. I expected a psychotherapist to understand that thinking and speaking of yourself as an ill person is never a story you want to tell. A big problem is you begin to play the starring role, building your story around that victim role. Take a moment now to PAUSE and PONDER the story you have been telling yourself. How does it make you feel?

I'm excited to share stories and wisdom from people I have great admiration for who have made positive shifts in their stories and are here to talk about the transformation.

Anne-Louise Sterry is a messenger of audacious joy. I asked her during our March 2011 interview at the 100th Anniversary of International Women's Day, "What do women need to know about achieving audacious joy?" Anne-Louise wanted me to know that just because she is a messenger of joy does not mean she doesn't get cranky every once in a while. Her transforming recipe for joy helps her spend much less time in cranky and much more time in happy.

Her recipe for joy starts with "live kindness" because it makes you feel good. It actually changes your brain and releases endorphins. She underlined that this doesn't mean only being kind to the people you like; it's being kind to everyone. Secondly, the joy recipe points to "embrace personal responsibility." Anne-Louise explained that it's her responsibility to take care of herself, her responsibility to bring happiness, and her responsibility to make positive changes in her life. She uses the word "embrace" because taking responsibility is a good thing, a powerful tool a woman can use for herself.

The final ingredient to achieve audacious joy is to choose a new story. You simply start with the words you tell yourself and the thoughts in your head. You can only hold one thought in your head at a time, so why don't you choose a happy one instead of a cranky one?

This simple recipe came from her personal exploration of living kindness to everyone, embracing personal responsibility and not feeling as though someone would always take care of her. Anne-Louise chose a new story, beginning with the cranky thoughts and concluding with the happy ones. Her comedic on-stage delivery of her material will raise the vibration in the entire room.

Based in Portland, Oregon, Anne-Louise speaks and performs nationally and internationally. She has released seven recordings of music, storytelling and personal development. Anne-Louise has a background in psychology, software training, nursing, education and performance, and is a member of numerous professional associations, including the National Speakers Association. She has taught storytelling for Portland State University and provides staff development programs for companies large and small. In April of 2013, Anne-Louise released her four CD Audio Course, "Rewire Your Brain for Audacious Joy," based on her work and experience.

Anne-Louise's repertoire is extensive and encompasses many genres from the sublime to the hilarious. Impossible to overlook is Aunt Lena, Anne-Louise's alter ego. A creation of Anne-Louise in the guise of everyone's out-of-the-box Italian relative, Aunt Lena mixes stories from the New Jersey homeland with cutting-edge Mediterranean wisdom. When Aunt Lena comes along with Anne-Louise, there's no telling what can happen! Check out more including "Aunt Lena's Cucina" a book written not just to show off her recipes, but to explain a little about how Aunt Lena looks at life, at Anne-Louise.com.

Anne-Louise says "live kindness." The Buddhists talk of "loving kindness." The Dalai Lama simply states, "My religion is very simple. My religion is kindness." Everyone appreciates kindness. In numerous studies, both men and women said kindness was the number one priority in their relationships.

So how about a new story of kindness for our relationships? After all, with a divorce rate of 67 percent in the U.S., it does appear that we could use some new ideas to change the relationship story.

With a background in genetic behaviorism and a series of workshops conducted in Marin County, California, Donna Sheehan and Paul Reffell are leading a cultural wakeup call by writing the groundbreaking book, "Redefining Seduction: Women Initiating Courtship, Partnership, and Peace." Donna and Paul are evolutionary psychologists who have done extensive research and have their own amazing relationship based on this theory. A premise of their work is that the egg chooses the sperm.

The story of the redefined seduction includes the following truths:
- Women, not men, should make the first move in courtship.

- Women's initiative in courtship is not only natural but essential to the survival of the species.

- Men are in awe of women.

- Every woman possesses the power to select and seduce her chosen mate.

Courage, confidence and grace come naturally to initiate courtship when you are tuned into your inner beauty, sensuality and sexuality. PONDER this new approach, and imagine how the world would be different. How does it make you feel to consider selecting a mate versus waiting for it to happen?

When enough people can envision and redefine old stories, then we have an opportunity to change the reality of the world. It calls for awareness and self-love so that you can live your truth with no regrets. The real you can PONDER and discern which part of the story you are living and which part was given to you. We are often living stories that others have created for us and can be completely unaware that this is the case. Our families, friends and teachers may have the best intentions, but only you know the story that will bring you to pleasure.

Nat Jones grew up in a show business family and was a child entertainer, making his first TV appearance at 4 years of age. He was an only child, avid reader and seeker of spirituality. He grew up believing that his truth was to become a successful actor, make lots of money and drive a jeep. When this story played out in Los Angeles as a young adult, with Nat starring in a regular TV series, earning great money and even driving the jeep, he felt something was terribly wrong. He became crippled by depression of how he thought he would feel if all of that were true.

Sixteen years after the initial recognition of his depression, he moved to Paris and found his authenticity on stage as a songwriter/singer in the jazz arena. How did he make that transition?

His deep desire to find his truth and the truth about life brought him to a poignant passage. It read, "Humans will always have pain, but the suffering is not necessary. The suffering is what we do when we are trying to avoid the pain." He worked with a skilled therapist for those 16 years guiding him, supporting him while he faced the feelings of sadness and helplessness from his childhood. Nat found his way to his authenticity by letting go of all the roles (and stories), and learned to just BE Nat Jones. Once he gave himself permission to feel his feelings, he began to understand that anger, sadness, happiness are all part of being human. He lived his life with complete openness where he allowed brokenness and not knowing to keep him connected to his higher self. He referred to it as surrendering to groundlessness.

Footnote

The world lost Nat Jones on September 22, 2013, as he waited to receive a heart transplant. I feel so blessed that I met him and he was moved to share his story with me. RIP Nat!

We have some pretty amazing survival stories. When you PONDER your survival story, there are traits and values that will emerge as meaningful in your life. We will look in the third part of "Healing with Pleasure Medicine: PULSE" at how you determine your values, how to capture the positive traits that you possess, and anchor them within.

It is empowering for women to hear other women's success and survival stories. Remember how popular Donna Summer's song "I Will Survive" was? There is a reason for it. We love it when women stand up for themselves. "As long as I've got love, I know I will survive..."

You've just read some very different examples of how the story you tell yourself really does matter. You have a unique story. What will you PONDER to make your story matter?

Rx from Chapter 6

1) PONDER how you feel about the story you tell yourself. Write your observations, without judgment, for 15 to 20 minutes in your journal.

2) What would your life be like if you surrendered to not knowing?

In the next chapter, we travel to France to PONDER the healing power of music with a group called "The Natural Healers."

Chapter 7

The Healing Power of Music

Music is pleasure. Music is healing. Music is healing with pleasure.

I have always had an appreciation for music, growing up as someone who loved to dance. Although I didn't grow up in Africa where you start listening and playing rhythms as soon as you are born, I did grow up with a mother and father who loved to sing. I can still picture my father dancing around the living room to Herb Alpert and the Tijuana Brass. He also loved to sing Christmas carols along with my mother. We had a whole repertoire of songs our family would sing in the car on vacations. So music has always been a part of my life growing up. I have seen the way it has changed the energy in my home when we would all start singing. It always felt good, and the family was having fun in a very connected way.

In Part 1 on Pause, I talked about my personal experience with Marvin Gaye and his hit, "Sexual Healing." Marvin's song has been rated as the number one song to get you in the mood for having sex. In addition, it has also been voted the track most likely to lead office workers to get frisky with one another at the office Christmas party, making it the most troublesome track, for the same reason, of course. There is no doubt that music will shift the energy in the room and change your mood.

In the summer of 2010, I traveled to Germany and France. I had an amazing time working with musicians for a live show and interviewing them about the healing power of music. When I look at all of the great interviews I have conducted, there are three main themes that have emerged.

First, musicians universally feel they could heal themselves emotionally and physically by playing their music. Secondly, the healing power of music stems from it being a universal form of communication. The final theme that emerged from these interviews was that music allows us to express difficult feelings in a safe way. Let's look a little closer at how these themes emerged for me. Along the way, I've got some great stories to share from these wonderful musicians.

When Yvette Summers and I designed the show "Living in Organic and Orgasmic Life," our highest intention was to bring healing on physical and emotional levels through story, music and dance. She discovered some musicians in Europe through Facebook, and they agreed to be a part of the project.

The first of these wonderful musicians was Inor Sotolongo, born in La Habana, Cuba, and now living in Paris. He began playing the congas at age 2. He told me that when he plays music, he forgets ALL. He said there is an energy so strong when he plays that any emotional or physical pain will go poof. Once he had a fever, and as soon as he started playing the fever disappeared. Inor believes he can heal anything through playing his music. He was a constant inspiration to me on this trip.

A second musician we spoke to was Fabrice Mareau, a gentleman who moved to France after growing up on the Caribbean island of Guadeloupe. He began playing percussion as a child because music was everywhere on the island. He said he was always tapping on something, as all the children in Guadeloupe play percussion. He said it's not serious, only for fun. He began playing the guitar when he saw a video of Prince and said to himself, "Oh yes, I want to do that, too."

When he moved to France, he had the blues and felt homesick for his grandmother, the food and the sea. Music was his way back to emotional balance. He said every time he played, he would feel better. In addition, his experience playing in hospital cancer units for children in Montpelier, France, proved to him that music heals. He said after two months of playing to the children on a weekly basis, they were smiling, singing and tapping.

Yet another musician we met was Ferricia Fatia. Ferricia is a ball of fire and passion who grew up in the United States and now lives in France as a singer and songwriter. She said, "We already know that harmonics are healing." But deeper than that, she believes it is sharing love through music that heals people. She urged music media to diffuse the violence of video music and turn to the music of love. She asked, "What if love was our science?"

Ferricia knows that music has the ability to bring us to the high vibration of love that is healing. She laughed and said we know all about songs of broken hearts, but we don't know what love is. Singing songs of love is a way to heal the people and the planet. Could it really be that simple?

We also met Yossi Fine, born to a West Indian singer and an Israeli guitar player. Yossi began playing the guitar at the age of 4. Whether as a producer, arranger or bassist, Yossi's unique and undeniable talents have made him one of the most in-demand names throughout a number of musical genres. Yossi told me that listening and playing music kept him from childhood depression. He said he lived with his grandmother and hated school. When he stayed home from school, he would play music all day long. It made him feel great. Yossi summed up his beliefs on the healing power of music, "The reason music heals is because we listen from our bodies; 70 percent with our bodies, 20 percent with our ears, and 10 percent with our eyes."

PONDER what is present for you when you sing, play an instrument or dance to some of your favorite music.

The fact of music being a universal form of communication showed up as I heard American music in numerous clubs, restaurants and stores in both France and Germany. Fa7's song "Carnaval" puts me in the same spirit as those who understand the lyrics. José Feliciano's version of "Feliz Navidad" gets me in a similar mood to the English version. Music rises above particular dialects and communicates in a global way. Can you feel the global nature of my time in Europe with this diverse group of artists? It is what truly gave me an appreciation for the universal nature of music.

Ayite was a fascinating African French musician Yvette and I became friends with while in Paris. He also grew up with roots firmly planted in music. He played the guitar at 9 years old.

He also said playing drums and singing was a natural experience for him growing up in his village in Africa. He said people in villages all around his house would play drums for someone who died and many other celebrations. There were always drums playing somewhere. Ayite plays his music mostly for other people and believes his main role is to entertain. When probed about the healing power of music, he agreed it's a healing and communication connection with the audience.

Meet Freddie Ravel, Founder of Human Harmonics. He is the internationally acclaimed Harmonics Maestro that blends his infectious passions for music and business to unlock the minds, hearts and hips of audiences around the world.

The #1 chart-topping keyboardist, speaker and producer is the creator of the unique Keynote Concert™ where strategic storytelling and customized music messaging merge to delight and inspire the greatness in leaders, teams and entrepreneurs alike.

Backed by number one hits and collaborative successes with Earth, Wind and Fire, Madonna, Prince, Indie Arie, Sergio Mendes, Quincy Jones, Al Jarreau, the Boston Pops and rock legend Carlos Santana, he is the Founder of Human Harmonics, the peak performance program to enhance leadership, innovation and collaboration within major companies and organizations. A few of his corporate clients include Starbucks, Coca-Cola, Toyota, Red Bull, NASA, Apple, Morgan Stanley, Google, and Citigroup.

As a one-of-a-kind "edutainer," Freddie is a captivating access point through which to transform entrepreneurs, events and companies forever.

He embodies the connection between music and science. Freddie says that every human responds to some rhythm. It's an ancient truth and a link to the way we listen to each other. His innovative program "Human Harmonics®" is a live keynote concert that blends a keynote talk on how music is related to our daily life. Through his methodology, Freddie illuminates that music is a multitasking power tool for life. You have your own melody to communicate to the world, harmonize with others to create teams. Freddie's program helps you rediscover your true inner rhythm so that you can manifest the "score" of your own life.

Music communicates to us by putting us in our bodies, where all the wisdom lives. When we can tune into our own inner rhythm and live from that place, we are in alignment with our souls. It doesn't matter where you live or what you look like because it is a universal experience.

Ti Harmon is a beautiful singer-songwriter originally from Philadelphia, now living in Paris. She said that music heals, in part, because it allows the singer to express sometimes difficult feelings. Her feelings are universally human, so often her audience has had similar experiences. This is yet another way music connects humans together. When you know you are not alone in your thoughts and feelings, you can relax and normalize your experience.

Ti knows how to have music help lift your spirit. She created a song called "Smile Today" while she was going through a particularly challenging time. She sings it every day in the mirror because it helps her project that her day will go in positive way. She experiences music as a positive energy field on the planet, and songs like "Smile Today" certainly contribute to that positivity. Her message is just that, stay in the positivity. These great lyrics will certainly get you started.

Smile Today

I ain't got no time

to be feeling sad

I'm just grateful for what I have

and I could sit, feeling shy

but it ain't gonna help me get by

I ain't got no time

to be feeling sad

I'm just grateful, grateful for what I have

and I could sit, feeling shy

or I could reach for the sky

Tell me now just what you think

don't you hold it all inside

Right or wrong don't matter

if you can't say what's in your heart today

So smile today

Find a way

It won't cause you any pain

And it's okay

Give thanks and pray

In the name of any name

I ain't got no time

to be feeling sad

I'm just grateful for what I have

and I could sit, feeling shy

or I could reach for the sky

I have relied on music to help me through some challenging times as well. It is a way to express feelings and shift the mood from sadness to appreciation and gratitude, as Ti's song above demonstrates. A few of my other favorites to start the day are the jazzy version of "Zippity Do Dah" by Patti LaBelle, "It's a Beautiful Morning" by The Rascals, and "Feel like a Woman" by Shania Twain.

• • •

Now clearly, I did not need to go to France to learn about the healing power of music. However, France has a very special acknowledgment of the importance of music. I was fortunate enough to be in Paris on June 21st, the summer solstice. Since 1982, France started holding the World Music Day invented by the French Minister of Culture, Jack Lang. Fete de la Musique is a celebration with music played all night on the streets and in clubs and restaurants throughout France. Both amateurs and professionals play all night long.

My Fete de la Musique experience started out at dinner where there was a Cuban band playing while we ate, and some got up and danced the salsa – the way those Cuban women can shimmy! WHOA Baby! After that we went to a rooftop salsa party until 2 a.m. On the way back to our apartment, the Metro was packed with partygoers. What a festive time it was. Sweaty people from all over the world, sticking together (literally), and music making it all happen.

Music is pleasure. Music gets us in our bodies. Music shifts energy. Music awakens our senses. Music and sound are healing.

Before I finish off this musical interlude into healing, let me share a groundbreaking technology using sound medicine.

Sandra Hickman is that CEO of Quantanomics, her entrepreneurial company. She is stewarding a unique and innovative device into the world that has the power to accelerate healing on the planet through capturing sound waves.

Sandra explains, "We have been going out in nature for years listening to the birds, the wind moving through the trees. Many have felt the healing qualities of these experiences. We have known that music has an amplitude of healing qualities for all sorts of things, from relaxation to reversing disease and illness. Our bodies are antennas, like an electrical system picking up vibrations all the time. And everything around is vibrating all the time."

Here is how her technology works: a unique substance, such as a homeopathic remedy, is entered into the special chamber device that isolates and amplifies the sound of the substance. What happens next is a unique vibrational signature of the substance is captured. Sandra does sound engineering to add in sounds of nature and harmonics. This results in a sound wave file (digital remedy) that can actually deliver the homeopathic medicine with a vibrational communication with the body. This is an alternative to taking a pill.

Sandra uses homeopathic remedies primarily because they get at the root cause of the problem and support healing. We know that taking pharmaceutical medication treats symptoms (not causes) and often suppresses your immune system.

Are you ready to try a sound healing process with the only side effect being relaxation? You can download a sample relaxation remedy at Sandra's website, sandrahickman.com.

Sandra's vision is that we all carry our digital medicine cabinet on our cell phones. This allows us to address our own self-healing whenever there is a need.

I challenge you to find your healing music and sound therapy. There's no right or wrong, it is just following your pleasure. Don't by shy, and reach for the sky! Thank you, Ti Harmon!

Rx from Chapter 7

1) Smile 10 times a day for no reason at all. Sing a few lines of Ti Harmon's song to yourself first thing in the morning.

2) Start your day with a 3 to 5 minute favorite song.

Do these for at least one week and record the "pleasure meter" results.

In Chapter 8, I will share my vision for the future of a healthy planet for your pondering pleasure.

Chapter 8

Future World to PONDER

One of my favorite questions to ask my radio or video guests is, "What is your vision of a healthy planet?" Their answers are always fascinating, and one of my purposes with this question is to paint the picture of what a healthy planet looks like so we can all PONDER it. And in our pondering, the chances of us creating that healthy planet increase. In this book on PONDER, let me share my personal answer to that question.

I hope by now that you are pondering a variety of ways to approach good health and well-being. I have presented a broad range of options from ancient wisdom's to cutting-edge technologies.

Surprise, surprise, MY vision of a healthy world includes women feeling beautiful, sensual and sexual. It is my belief that this sacred part of a woman's nature can create healing for our relationships and our earth.

Let's take a look at how I came to this conclusion.

Source: Bulletin of Experimental Biology and Medicine

"Sex increases the hormone oxytocin. As the oxytocin surges, endorphins increase and pain declines. So if your headache, arthritis pain or PMS symptoms improve after sex, thank oxytocin."

Although this appeared in the Bulletin of Experimental Medicine, orgasms have been used in medicine to treat female hysteria since at least the 1850s. Don't believe anything you don't want to, AND it might be worth a try to consider regular natural sex (which might be anywhere on the spectrum from mental orgasms to intercourse). I will explain mental orgasms and channeling sexual energy in the third book in the series, PULSE. But for now, PONDER the idea of having sex instead of taking toxic medication. The side effects of sex are pleasure.

It may not be the cure-all for pain and many other health conditions; however, it is certainly a handy adjunct to any therapies you may be using.

Women need to learn about their bodies to create a different relationship in their sex lives. It is difficult for many of us to use the words orgasm, clitoris and vagina. When I grew up, we didn't even call the vagina by its name. We called it a "tooney." I don't even remember when I first learned the correct name for the body part.

From my experience in speaking to many different groups about orgasm, I've come to understand the word itself gets a wide variety of reactions. My favorite is the MS support group I spoke to, and as soon as I said the word orgasm, a woman in the back of the room yelled, "I love orgasms." I have also spoken to a group of progressive thinkers in Northern California who tensed every time I said the word orgasm. You never know how people will respond, and my vision for the future is that the word orgasm conjures up the juiciest and yummiest of feelings within a human body without any guilt or embarrassment.

We can get a glimpse of why it hasn't been easy to embrace our sexuality and all the pleasure that goes with it when you look at this article written by the blog.museumofsex.com on "The Internal Clitoris."

"Consider this: In over 5 million years of evolution, only one organ has come to exist for the sole purpose of providing pleasure, the clitoris. It is not required in reproduction; it doesn't have a urethra running through it like the penis, and thus does not urinate. Its sole function, its singular wonderful purpose, is to make a woman feel good. Sadly, because the clitoris has no function except for female pleasure, science has neglected to study it as intricately as the penis."

That's a WHOA Baby in my book.

We are not studying an organ because its sole purpose is to bring a woman pleasure?! Now I'll take a quick moment to go political here, to keep us aware of why we have pain with our sexuality. There is the horrible incidence of the genital mutilation of young girls that I would be naive not to mention here. Female genital mutilation is practiced as a cultural ritual by ethnic groups in 27 countries in Sub-Saharan and Northeast Africa. It is most often performed on a girl under the age of 5. That is the extreme example of how we fear the power of a sexual woman. This is so painful to PONDER.

One more point of pain is that the medical system has not studied the woman's body with the same verve as a man's body. Dr. Louann Brizendine, MD, author of "The Female Brain," shared with me that her college professor told her the pill was studied on the male brain because the female hormones would screw up the data.

They have learned that the clitoris extends deep within, not just the bulb at the opening of the vagina. It's got eight thousand sensory nerves, which is twice the number of nerves that a penis has.

In 1998, Dr. Helen O'Connell from Melbourne University published her findings of the size of the clitoris after microscopically examining the nerve ends. Men's penises have been examined in depth as early as the 1970s. Interestingly, that same year of Dr. O'Connell's findings about the size of the clitoris, men started popping Viagra for erectile dysfunction.

In 2009, the first 3-D sonographs were used to see how far the clitoris extended. It was the French who made this discovery. Two French physicians spoke out about the medical literature and its contempt for women. One physician was quoted as saying, "The very existence of an organ of pleasure is denied medically. In a surgeon's text, there are two pages on the clitoris. There is an intellectual excision."

So PONDER this: We go to our doctors to have them help us feel good, and they don't even know about the pleasure organ in our body.

Ladies, we need to charter a new path. We need to take responsibility for learning about our bodies and what brings our wonderful, fabulous, beautiful and unique bodies pleasure. It will be marvelous for you, AND it's a life-or-death situation for our planet.

Women connecting with their bodies on a soul-level are where the miracles of pleasure healing happen. A Tantric teacher I worked with told me that it is possible for women to be orgasmic 24/7. Imagine a life where everything you do comes from love and brings you pleasure. It is an inner state that could be thought of as your highest self in your truest nature.

Well, I started off with my ultimate vision. What is needed to get us there is to develop an intimate relationship with sensuality and beauty. My supporting visions will paint the picture of women living in their beauty, finding deep gratitude in the joy of their senses, and living in the moment.

I lived in Seattle, Washington, for a few months last year, and found it one of the most beautiful cities in the world. The "Emerald City" is known for its dark green foliage and the small city parks sprinkled all over. The view of Puget Sound, the ferries traveling to the surrounding islands at night and the snow-covered Olympic Mountains create in orgasmic feast for one's eyes.

I used to walk to one of those sweet little city parks, where I found a bench tucked way back in the trees. On the bench was a plaque that read, "A respite, for those who see beauty in all things." You can imagine how at home I felt sitting on this bench.

Why is it so easy to feast our eyes on the beauty in these scenes in nature, yet so hard to feast our eyes on the beauty that stares back at us in the mirror? We really know the reasons. Our media has exposed us to impossible images, and even those models that come close to the 5-foot-9, 120 pounds, with long hair and gorgeous skin don't feel beautiful.

This must change. The fact that only 3 percent of women world-wide can comfortably call themselves beautiful is one of the most detrimental things to our planet. If we don't feel our own beautiful self to cherish and love, the beauty and love that lives on the outside is all illusion. This is what I want women to start pondering and learning to PULSE out into the world.

What we would not hear if women felt beautiful:

Do I look fat in these jeans?

I'm having a bad hair day.

You like this old rag? It is so faded and ugly.

My boyfriend is the one who makes me feel beautiful.

I hate my thighs.

What we would hear, if women felt beautiful:

Thank you, I love this dress on me, too, even though I have had it forever.

Said to self: I love you in all the beautiful ways you express yourself.

Looking in your eyes: you are a beautiful soul.

Every inch of my body is luscious, and orgasmic, I might add.

When I feel my beauty, those around me seem to feel more beautiful, too.

This is for you, all of your relationships, and our desperate planet.

What many of my clients have reported when they begin to develop this more intimate relationship with their own beauty is their sense of sight becomes more heightened and they notice beauty all around them. Those moments of sensuality where you stop, breathe and bring your full attention to the sunset, a child's face, or the blooming flower brings you to a sense of deep gratitude and appreciation. That takes the pleasure meter to a new level.

Yes, this is what sensuality contributes to our lives: The ability to come alive in any moment that you choose to focus 100 percent attention on one of your senses. Do you feel the power?

Sensuality, and allowing the aliveness of sensuality in your life, is all about awareness. You know the experience. It's when one of your senses kicks in and your attention is pulled to experience it more fully. I am fortunate enough to live in a house where great yummy food is always prepared. There are many times that I have walked into the house and a wonderful aroma greets me. When I walked into the house, I might've been thinking about what I was going to do next or my last experience, and then all of my attention turns to the scent of what is being prepared. In those moments, I practice what I preach. I stop and breathe and appreciate the chef preparing the meal and enjoy the aromatherapy that is available.

I could give you examples like these for each one of our other senses of sound, taste and touch. Instead, I will make it part of the prescription for this chapter. You can find the examples in your own life. Not only is it more meaningful for you, but you also see that it exists for you.

When I imagine a world where sensuality is prevalent, what I see are smiling faces and lots of PAUSING.

Marion Williamson writes in her book "A Return to Love,"

> "When Michelangelo was asked how he created a piece of sculpture, he answered that the statue already existed within the marble. He said God himself had created that Pieta, David, and Moses. Michelangelo's job, as he saw it, was to get rid of the excess marble that surrounded God's creation. Your job is to remove the fearful thinking that surrounds your perfect self, just as excess marble surrounded Michelangelo's perfect statue."

Isn't it time to remove the excess (protective layer) and reveal the beautiful, sensual and sexual woman that you are?

PONDER THAT

Rx from Chapter 8

1) Google "clitoris" and explore yours.

2) Find moments in your life where you have been tuned into and feeling the pleasure of each of your five senses.

The final chapter in this section on PONDER is about taking quantum leaps. Is it your time to leap into who you really are in your soulful core?

* * *

Chapter 9

Moving to Pleasure, Part II

What makes a life extraordinary?

What do you think? Lots of money, fame or accomplishments may be the first place you think to look. Whoops...not there!

I would like to offer that we ALL live extraordinary and ordinary lives right in this moment. Each and every one of us has that unique combination of amazingness that no one else has. That makes us far from ordinary. The paradox of wanting to belong and be accepted AND wanting to self-express keeps us in a conundrum of how to really feel about the BEing inside.

How can we fill ourselves up with the best of who we are and bring that beautiful self to our relationships? To our planet? How can we have organic, orgasmic relationships that are based in honesty and acceptance? Okay, Coach Betty, enough with the questions!

Well folks, that is exactly how you get to the place of healing with pleasure medicine, by PONDERING meaningful questions that allow you to safely look at how you are living your life without judging it. That is what the first two books in this series have been all about. Giving you an opportunity to explore pleasure in a way that will help you integrate and live it, not just think or talk about it.

The path to pleasure may not feel comfortable. If you have been someone who prepares for the worst and tends to look for what's wrong instead of what's right, moving to pleasure is out of your comfort zone. Yet that is where so many of your own unanswered questions live.

My friend and mentor, Olga Aura, says to be a master of your destiny, you need to be able to take action in spite of doubt and fear. It may mean leaving behind everything you know and taking a leap to something different. Olga knows a little bit about taking leaps, as she was a gold medal gymnast from the Ukraine who came to the Olympics in America and did not get back on her bus. She did not speak English and had no job. She said it was the calling in her soul that made her take the leap. At that time, Olga was an extraordinary gymnast on the outside, but she was crawling on her knees in the dark on the inside.

You may have experienced that at some point in your life, too. You may have had situations where it is so uncomfortable to stay in the job, relationship, friendship, etc., and yet you know it is going to stretch you out of your comfort zone to change. My strong urge for you is to take the new road. Don't keep walking down the same path expecting something different. You know that is called insanity.

Olga's thoughts on quantum leaps revolve around the notion that you are no longer asked to take small steps. She describes this communication as taking place in the territory of the soul. She said in order for her to stay in America, she connected with the inner spiritual plasma, or fire of the soul, and let that power her. Does that sound juicy or what?

Again, we talk about letting go of the old so the new can emerge. Maybe holding a funeral service for the old you, as Olga suggests, is appropriate.

This calling of mine, the calling of living lives of pleasure, stems from my connection with the earth. My vision is that as women discover this juicy place of inner beauty, sensuality and sexuality, Mother Earth is going to feel juicy, filled up and nurtured as well. We are feminine energy. Mother Earth is feminine energy. If we are dried up and unhappy, how can Mother Earth thrive?

When have you arrived at pleasure? How do you know you are using pleasure medicine to heal?

The final section in this book, "Healing with Pleasure Medicine: PULSE," will go in detail to help you see and feel the arrival of pleasure in your life.

Rx from Chapter 9

1) Choose the most meaningful question from the list below. PONDER and write about it for the next month.

2) Consider what your vision of a life with pleasure looks like. Ask for help.

LIFE QUESTIONS

What has to happen before I would consider my life fulfilled?

What are my biggest obstacles to receiving from others?

What holds you back from BEing magnificent?

What is your evidence that pleasure heals?

How much do you live in your head? Your body?

How compassionate are you with yourself?

PART 3

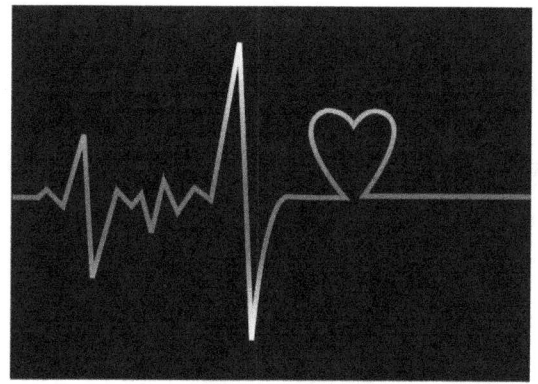

PULSE

Chapter 1

The Wisdom of Your Body

You know the wisdom of your body. Your body tells you when it's hungry, sleepy, excited, unhappy, or any other emotion or feeling. Most of us have had the experience of overriding our body's messages, and then the wisdom of the body is lost.

For me, this is seen in my ability to override the whispers of pain when my body is telling me to rest. But the to-do list says, "You can't rest today, there is way too much to do." You can probably guess what happens next. Either I have so much pain that I must rest, or I'm too exhausted to handle any of the to-do list.

You may have experienced overriding a body message with either sleep or food. Have you ever waited a long time to eat because either you didn't know what to eat or it wasn't convenient? I remember one vacation as a child when my sister did this on a family car trip. She didn't eat enough and then kept saying it was okay, she could make it until dinner-time. In addition, she was a super picky eater. We always had to find a restaurant that served spaghetti and meatballs.

On this particular trip, we searched for a while and finally found a pasta place for dinner, only to discover the wait for a table was an hour. As my sister sat there waiting, her body started to shut down. The next thing we knew, she had slumped over and fainted. Her body would not go on any more without food.

One good thing came out of it: we didn't have to wait an hour for a table as soon as the hostess saw she had fainted. Once she had some dinner, she was fine. By the way, I don't recommend this as a way to bypass the wait at a busy restaurant.

Most people have experienced this body phenomenon with sleep, since over 50 percent of the population is sleep deprived. Our bodies can be stretched and pulled and propped up for a long time, but they eventually will shut down in some capacity if you do not pay attention. Listen for those whispers. Listening for those whispers gets you deeply in touch with the wisdom of the body AND allows you to experience pleasure.

That means relaxation. Relaxation reduces stress and opens you up to many new possibilities of embracing your deeper beauty, sensuality and sexuality. It also has a big effect on health conditions such as chronic pain. The National Institutes of Health says stress is the cause of 70 percent of our health conditions. It makes sense.

We cannot discuss the wisdom of our bodies without a conversation about the wisdom of women rediscovering their beauty, inside and out. I can not say this enough: When women are in touch with their beauty, everyone wins. When they are not in touch with their beauty, everyone loses.

The importance of repeating this throughout this series of books serves as a constant reminder of this truth. We have focused on the negative for so long. I heard a real WHOA Baby at the 100th celebration of International Women's Day in 2011. There were speakers from all over the country talking about how women have become more powerful. However, one area of our lives in which we give up our power is the way we feel about our bodies.

These are some quotes from Tamilee Webb of Exercise TV and the famous video series, "Buns of Steel" and "Abs of Steel"."

"97 percent of women do not like something about their bodies!"

"68 percent of women feel worse about how they look when they page through women's magazines."

"90 percent of women overestimate their body size."

Tamilee mentioned that when she was in her twenties, she did not like her body. Now that she is in her fifties, she would love to have that 20-year-old body back. When will we learn to love our bodies? When you do not feel good about yourself, no matter how hard you try, you do not bring good energy onto the planet. You see, everybody loses because you don't like the way you look! How can you be in your true womanly power if you are concerned about cellulite or looking fat or or or? The list is quite huge, as you know.

You are a beautiful soul that has a beautiful spirit and juicy body. It does not make anyone happy that you are not happy with you.

This is for your happiness, all the people in your life, AND our world! Yes, we can overcome the insanity of women not recognizing the power of their own beauty.

Speaking of insanity, let's look at women and their connection to their sexuality. As I continue to read and learn more on this topic of women sexuality, I find more evidence of the connection between beauty and sexuality. Thomas Moore writes in his book, "The Soul of Sex: Cultivating Life as an Act of Love," that true beauty casts a spell. It is the work of magic and serves sexuality because it offers pleasure and gives rise to the desire for union.

My friend and kindred spirit, Monica Day, founder of SensualLife.com, takes it deeper and writes, "Orgasm is the basis of all life. It is the most powerful energy that lives within every single one of us, and between us when we come together in sensual relationships. In popular culture, we have labeled the climax of a sexual experience an orgasm, and yet orgasmic energy is much more expansive, available and abundant than just these moments. Our ability to feel pleasure, sensation, connection and love is endless when we enter the gateway of our orgasm."

Monica specializes in creating safe spaces for people to explore, experience and express their sensuality. She is best-known for finding playful ways to engage people into exploring what it means to live a more feeling, passionate, fully expressed sensual life. She has spent the last 18 years as a writer, trainer and facilitator in areas ranging from personal growth and awareness, race and gender, class and power, sensuality and sexuality, to communication skills and relationship dynamics. The Sensual Life is Monica's vehicle for sharing with others the tools of deeper communication, the turn-on of sensual awareness, and the practices that arouse greater freedom, awakening, love and spiritual connection.

I love the way she talks about sensuality. She describes sensuality as something we experience through the senses, where we notice more emotional feelings and are willing to feel more in every aspect of life. This adds more spice to our sexual energy.

Sensuality is not linear. Many people have a hard time perceiving or opening up to the idea that things are related, even when they don't seem connected, because it requires them to take experiences out of the box. It means allowing experiences to be more fluid.

Monica, too, had a message about how women feel about their bodies. For that fulfilling and sacred sexual experience, you need to fully enter into agreement with what is your body. Then you can relax.

Monica has been doing this work for many years, so I asked her what transformation she notices when women are willing to risk out-of-the-box thinking. She answered that self-confidence shoots way up. We see the beauty in ourselves and start to look at us like a lover would. We are so much more attractive when we feel we are the most fabulous thing, and the result is confidence. If you don't want to be with yourself, why would someone else want to be with you?

To top off the interview with vintage Monica, she said, "We, as women, believe someone gives you an orgasm. You are born with your orgasm. You can share it along with everything energetically inside of you. You own your orgasm. Don't look for the person to find the magic button. You find it."

I know I have mentioned the healing qualities of sex before. It has been sprinkled throughout this series of books. Here is yet another WHOA Baby from the radio show which opened my eyes again to real evidence that sex can heal common conditions such as headaches very effectively.

A team of neurologists found that sexual activity can lead to "partial or complete relief" of head pain in some migraines. The study, from the University of Münster, Germany, suggests that instead of using a sore head as an excuse to refuse sex, making love can be more effective than taking painkillers.

Their research, reported in *Cephalalgia*, the journal of the International Headache Society, found that more than half of migraine sufferers who had sex during an episode experienced an improvement in symptoms.

One in five patients left without any pain at all, while others, in particular male sufferers, "even used sexual activity as a therapeutic tool," they added.

Neurologists suggested that sex triggered the release of endorphins, the body's natural painkillers, through the central nervous system. This can reduce or even eliminate a headache.

Can you imagine a world where we look to our sexuality as a part of our medicine?

Recall that in the 1850s, Victorian physicians performed vaginal massage (orgasm) to treat female hysteria. The movie *Hysteria* documents this time in history, which led to the invention of the vibrator.

I have also been vocal about sexual wellness as a natural way to improve your immune system, cardiovascular system and overall well-being. This sounds like body wisdom to me.

What makes us resistant and hesitant to embrace this?

In my research and experience coaching women about their sexuality, I have identified the following reasons we resist the power of sexual healing:

Religious Training – Interpretations of sex and sexual behavior by many religions teaches repression and shame. This has created confusion in enjoying sex for both young and mature women alike. If you are unable to enjoy sex, it will not be a healing experience.

Reliance or Dependence on a Quick Fix – Our trained response when we have a health issue is to see a doctor or take a pill. When is the last time you were ill and thought sex could help? We are greatly influenced by the abundance of advertised pharmaceuticals.

Belief Systems – We have not been exposed enough to the belief that sex can relieve pain and be healing, even though Marvin Gaye's music has communicated this for more than thirty years. Our belief systems are formed by our experiences, and they can change in a moment.

The good news is the seed has now been planted. Consider the side effects of orgasm the next time you have a headache.

Here is one more point, for now, I want to make on body wisdom. I do feel I could write volumes on this topic. Our bodies are the very best guide to show us what is meaningful and important in terms of our core values, talents, skills and general JUICE for life.

It is so simple. If your body is relaxed and feeling good, your mind positive and your spirit light, then you are honoring your values, skills, talents and your unique life purpose.

The reverse is also true. If you are tense, thinking half-empty thoughts, exhausted, heavy energy, living in the past or future, then you are not in alignment with who you are at your core. No matter what the circumstances of why you feel you need to do what you are doing, the truth is you are not honoring your inner core values and your body will tell you. Your body wants you to be in alignment with who you are.

It is my intention to guide you through this process of moving to that more honoring place seemlessly through this series of books and other support materials.

The next chapter goes right for self-pleasure.

Rx from Chapter 1

1) Take 30 seconds right now to identify something you love about the way you look. Find at least three ways to accent that body part in the next week.

2) Before you get up each morning and before you go to sleep, take a 30-second body scan and see if your body is whispering to you.

Chapter 2

Self-Pleasure

I recently invited a client to consider the following question: How can you make it all about you without feeling guilty? That pondering question, combined with a request to make a list of 20 ways to love yourself, produced the following response from her the next week. She said, "There are many ways that I show myself love. I guess I really do love myself!"

The last chapter emphasized that if women feel good, then friends, family, and even the planet feel good. This chapter is all about the ways we can find self-pleasure within our current situations and lives. I would not be surprised if many of you would have the same response as my client did. You may love yourself more than you think you do.

By now, you know that I am always a fan of the simple. How can we break things down so they feel doable and easy? Finding pleasure does not mean you have to go on a fancy vacation to an exotic location. It means becoming aware of what brings you pleasure and then becoming very present with those times, leaning into the pleasure that is available.

For instance, when you are taking a shower, give yourself an extra minute to become present with the warm water pulsing over your body. Most women I know find this a very pleasurable thing to do. When you are out of the shower, take care and love to spread lotion all over your body as a lover might do. That is how simple it can be. You are already doing the activities, so it is a matter of your attention and focus.

Key Point: Pleasure is a way of thinking.

Now let's look at the self-pleasure of sexuality. I am amazed with all I have learned about the health benefits of having regular loving and consensual sex, whether it is with another person or yourself.

Dr. David Weeks, from Scotland's Edinburgh Hospital, studied 3,500 Americans and Europeans from ages 18-102, and found that only 25 percent of youthful looks is due to genetics. The rest of youthful looks is related to behavior. When he examined sexual behavior, he found that having sex three times a week can make you look a decade younger.

Check out the whole article, Vitamin S:
"http://www.winnipegfreepress.com/life/vitamin-s-116145664.html"

Sex as a healing modality is ancient wisdom. It packs a powerful punch of goodness when we understand and believe in its positive effects. Sex is a positive force of goodness in our world when we understand and carry it out for healing and sacred communion. It is so good for our health and there are no insurance premiums. Plus, we carry this healing power around with us wherever we go.

Doesn't that make it worthwhile to investigate further how you can bring more soulful and sacred sex into your life?

The first step to this kind of fabulous sex is to fall in love with yourself!

I am going to share a very vulnerable story with you now which proved to me that self-love creates an opening for some beautiful experiences sexually. I share these stories to give you an idea as to what is possible for you.

I am one of the lucky women who never had too much trouble coming to an orgasm. My first lover was much older than I and was quite an expert at finding the G-spot. He slowly and tenderly taught me how much pleasure my body could bring. I was enamored with him and thought he was the greatest lover. My experience with men for the next 30 years after that found me having really good sex and thanking my lovers profusely for their talent. Little did I know at that time that it was my ability to relax, allow, and surrender that made the sex so good.

After my daughter left for college, I moved into a little house by myself in Northern California. This was the first time in over 30 years that I lived by myself. I consciously planned that this was my time to fall in love with me. I spent lots of time in that house on my own, and this is where I discovered the many ways to love myself without feeling the least bit guilty.

My life was feeling really good from the inside and I wanted to enjoy the company of men again, so I started dating this very nice man. I could feel how much more protective I was of my own space and time. However, he was persistent. One night he came over and offered to give me a massage on the floor in front of the fireplace. How romantic, right? Because loving yourself means allowing yourself to receive pleasure, I said that I would love that. For the next three hours he massaged and touched me, and brought me to orgasm numerous times. I was so relaxed, content and at peace.

The biggest takeaway from this story is he spent all that time bringing me pleasure, and I did not "take care of him" sexually at all. He made it all about me, and I allowed it to be. The real surprise for me came when he went to sleep that night with the biggest smile on his face.

Self-love and self-pleasure go hand in hand. Falling in love with yourself means figuring out where you are on the Personal Pleasure Meter.

Pleasure is so much about awareness. When you are aware that there is something called a pleasure meter and gauge your own pleasure in any given moment, then your attention toward pleasure is there and increases because you are thinking about it. How cool is that?

Use this as a game with your friends and family. Get the whole room talking about their pleasure meter and what makes pleasure meters go off their charts, and you will see a room come alive.

I had the honor of speaking to a cancer support group about the Ps of Peace, Passion and Pleasure. I shared some of the stories I am sharing with you now, and by the end of the meeting, everyone was sharing orgasm stories. It cracked me up. The whole room was buzzing, and this one woman pulled me aside and said, "I didn't want the whole group to hear this, but I wanted to tell you. When I got out of my first mastectomy surgery and they were wheeling me to radiation and chemo, and I was laying on the gurney in the hospital hallway and all these medical people were buzzing around me, I wanted to transport myself to another time and place so I decided to bring myself to orgasm. So right there with no one paying attention to me, that is exactly what I did. And every time I think of that story, I smile." That is the power of orgasmic energy, channeling it anytime, anyplace and anywhere.

I have spent the lion's share of this series talking about going inward and truly learning who you are as a beautiful, sensual and sexual being. This chapter completes that journey, for now, and the rest of this third and final book will focus on you channeling and stepping forward as the magnificent being you are.

The world needs your beautiful, juicy energy. You are ready, no matter where you are, because there is always more to learn. You don't have to have it perfect when you express yourself to the world. The more imperfect, the better ... because here we are talking about being totally and completely human.

Now let's explore how to PULSE our magnificent humanness out to the world.

Rx from Chapter 2

1) Every morning, for the next month, Pause, Look in the Mirror, and ask "Who Loves Ya, Baby?"

2) For the next week, gauge your pleasure meter every night before bed.

Chapter 3

Meet, Point, Dance

We do not want to hide our magnificence. As we go through this process of self-discovery and sink deeper into our beauty, sensuality and sexuality, we get to share the goods with everyone, and especially those women coming up behind us. As we are shifting into more divine feminine consciousness, we want our young women to be prepared. That means whether you are young or old, if you are in touch with your deeply sacred feminine being, your commitment to PULSING that out there in the world can create a domino effect and help heal the planet.

Don't be afraid. We are all learning how to do it. There is no rulebook for how we bring it all into balance. What I know is it is much simpler than we make it. It is a returning to who we were meant to be, and it means you are stepping into a Bigger Game.

There is a brilliant life coach and leader, Rick Tamlyn, who co-created the workshop and organization The Bigger Game in 2001 as a way to inspire executives, leaders and individuals to get out of their comfort zones and invent the lives they want. At its core, The Bigger Game helps people find their compelling purpose. It is an innovative model that guides you to create a set of circumstances that will intentionally design who you want to become, and it is definitely worth checking out. Look in the Resources section for the website.

The reason I bring up The Bigger Game now is that the concept of meet, point and dance comes from its model and training. As we bring our new selves out into the world, we need to remember that everyone else has not been doing the inner work and exploration. Compassion and patience is needed for you and your loved ones as we transition to new ways of Being in the world.

The concept works like this:

- Meet them where they are.
- Point them to the new healthier vision.
- Dance with them.

The "them" could be your spouse, parents, children, colleagues, or other family and friends. When you are breaking ground to new ways of thinking and Being, this is an important skill to have under your belt.

Let me demonstrate this through a couple radio show stories about meet, point and dance. First, I will introduce you to Titilayo Adedokun, who did a fabulous meet, point and dance with herself. I'll follow that up with sexuality medicine specialists Drs. Lana Holstein and David Taylor, who offer places to meet, point and dance in our romantic relationships.

Titilayo Adedokun has a story of meeting herself where she was, going toward a new vision, and dancing her magnificence out into the world while making a wonderful contribution to humanity.

She was born in the U.S. (Midwest) to Nigerian parents and now lives in Munich, Germany. You will see how she used her beauty and magnificence to PULSE something very wonderful in the world.

This woman is a former Miss Ohio, former runner-up to Miss America, and learned early that the universe knew more than she knew. Even though she loved a life of structure, going with the flow led to her founding a philanthropic organization.

Titilayo is very smart, starting college at the ripe young age of 14. She was a law student who had joined the college choir because she had been singing in her father's church even before speaking. However, being one of five children, her parents could not keep up with the finances of a college education.

Since she was such a great singer, the college offered her to pay full tuition if she became a music major. She did, and graduated with a double major. It truly was a moment of universal guidance, as she never pursued law, instead becoming a professional singer and actress. "No experiences are wasted," Titilayo said.

There are three gems of wisdom I want to underline from this talented and dynamic woman.

First, she emphasized that based on her own experience, we do not necessarily know what direction our lives should take. When a hindrance comes down, it is the universe directing.

Secondly, she said when you lose direction of your own life, do something outside of yourself, look to who needs help. She was adamant about women helping women. She started a community of women in Germany for a dosage of support. They would meet every two weeks. There, she was not her own center of attention. They would put their heads together and make things happen for each other. Collaboration at its finest.

Finally, she shared the story of how a visit to Africa resulted in her and her husband starting a scholarship fund for two schools. This came on the tails of her disgust with the way of the town and run of the schools they had witnessed. Titilayo initially just wanted to leave and never come back. Her husband stopped her and said, "We need to see how we can help so we are not part of the problem." They went home and found incredible support from friends and family who wanted to sponsor children, and then added another school to the foundation.

Titilayo found her compelling purpose by being open to the universe, and then she PULSED her beauty, sensuality and sexuality out into the world through her natural talent for singing and her huge heart. Isn't it exciting what is possible when we listen and follow the flow?

You have PAUSED and PONDERED, and you have a better idea of who the beautiful, sensual, sexual being is inside of you. PULSING that into your primary relationship can be a place for lots of meeting, pointing and dancing. Drs. Lana Holstein and David Taylor provide a framework of the seven dimensions of sexuality medicine to help you with those dances.

Examining these dimensions, you can begin to see what you need to allow for sex to become multi-dimensional, sacred and fulfilling. Each one of these dimensions offers a place to meet, point and dance with your primary sexual partner.

Biologic - Bodies and functions as living organisms

Sensual - Ability to feel and perceive pleasure

Desire - What some think of as sexiness or lust

Heart - Exchange love and commitment

Intimacy - Revealing ourselves with truth and trusting the other person

Aesthetic - Appreciating and revealing radiance to other person

Ecstatic - Blend with another human being and connect with the higher powers

How can you open up a discussion with your primary partner or someone safe about what you want and need around sexuality in any one of these dimensions? Start with one and explore it fully. Review Chapter 4 in Part 1 ("Pause"), "Ask for What you Want and Need." If this feels like a big leap to take. What I like about dissecting this topic into dimensions is it always is easier to meet someone where they are when you narrow down the issue. Whether you are meeting yourself or another person, be specific.

Another takeaway from this concept of meet, point and dance is that when you are healing and re-discovering who you really are at your core, there might be misunderstandings between you and your loved ones. They might feel you pulling away from who they know you to be.

Meeting their understanding is key to making the transition harmoniously. Say things like, "I understand I am thinking and doing things differently." Let them know how it feels to be stepping into a Bigger Game. It may even open them up to their own Bigger Game. The bigger vision is for all of us to step into our Bigger Games.

Finally, you know it wouldn't be Coach Betty Louise if I didn't remind you that even though we are PULSING ourselves outward, the most important person for you to meet, point and dance with is you. If you don't know your beautiful, sensual and sexual nature, then you have nothing positive to PULSE.

In the next chapter, we shall explore the PULSE of your sensual energy and how you can channel it to ordinary experiences.

Rx from Chapter 3

1) Choose a circumstance in your life where you want to influence someone to see what you see. Use the meet, point, dance concept.

2) Open up a deeper discussion about your own sexual medicine by picking one of the seven dimensions outlined by Drs. Holstein and Taylor. Discuss it with the safest person in your life, whether it is a lover or not.

Chapter 4

Channeling Sensual Energy Into Ordinary Experiences

There is an energy system within all of us. Understanding our energy system helps us PULSE our vibration outward. It involves intangible concepts which require you to open your mind to new possibilities. I spoke with Mat Stein, a scientist from Truckee, Calif., about he opened his mind and learned how we can use our chakra energy system.

I have worked with many alternative healers and learned that energy medicine works on the physical, mental, emotional and spiritual bodies. By the time we manifest a disease, the issue has been living in one of the energy bodies for a long time. That means the healing could take a long time.

The chakras are how our spiritual body interacts with our physical body. This happens primarily through the endocrine glands. The Sanskrit meaning for chakra is "a wheel that spins," so the chakras are considered spinning wheels of electro-magnetic energy. When we learn how to work with the chakras, our alignment of chakra energy is what creates wellness.

One way to think about it is that the spiritual body is the least dense and most ethereal, the thought body little more dense, the emotional body more dense, and the physical body is matter and very dense. So we start to move the energy in the spiritual body, and the physical body is the last to respond.

This tracks what my experience with pain has been. I recognize old patterns to let go, forgive myself, and align my thoughts and emotions with the new reality. For those changing energies to create a difference in my physical pain … well, let's just say it takes a while.

Chakras are centers of spiritual power in the human body. They are real, but not tangible to most people. That is why I asked Mat Stein, MIT grad and author of "When Technology Fails," to share his experience with the chakras, because he includes this information in his book. Imagine if technology were to fail, we would need to rely on medicines other than running to the pharmacy. Here is what Mat said about the chakra system:

"There is still so much science does not understand. Western medicine does not understand what controls health for humans. Eastern medicine has explored wellness through the perspective of spirit. What we know is that energy centers are critical to our wellness and maintaining health. Just because western scientists can't explain it doesn't mean it isn't real."

His story goes something like this. When working in California as an MIT intern, Mat read about a 108-year-old yogi and the miraculous healing he performed. His fingers started shaking, and he became compelled to visit this man in India.

Mat's western science mind was shattered when he saw this man. Prior to that meeting, he thought everything could be explained by science. He was sent around cosmos, and his science mind was blown. After the experience, Mat became much more open to spiritual possibilities. He now has some amazing, personally experienced stories of natural healing.

There is a lot of information on the internet about chakras, and I am far from an expert, but I do want to give you some basic information.

Remember a chakra is a Sanskrit word meaning "wheel that spins," and it refers to vortexes of energy, spinning like wheels in the body. The chakras are our spiritual organs, processing energy and vibrations much like our physical organs process food and water. They are located deep within the center of the physical body along the spinal column.

Each chakra corresponds to different glands and organs of the body. They draw in the divine life-force energy from the universe and distribute this vital energy to the glands and organs for optimum health and well-being.

When our chakras are balanced, maximum vitality and health is experienced. Physical or emotional trauma will affect the corresponding chakra. Balancing our chakras can be accomplished in a number of ways; for example, through the healing arts, guided meditation, or the use of energy manipulation in the auric fields. Other useful techniques thought to balance chakras and create the state of well-being are Chakra Balancing, Inner Child Retrieval, Intuitive/Spiritual Counseling, Spiritual Healing, and Past Life Regression.

There are seven primary chakras, and each has an associated color.

Balancing Chakras

Here is my framework for balancing and setting chakras. If you are inspired and intrigued, please explore further. Find words, ideas and thoughts about energy, chakras and auras that land for you and feel right in your gut.

Working with your energy system involves setting intentions and visualizing the steps below:

1. Ground yourself by sending a cord from the base of your spine down to the center of the earth.

2. Open the chakras at the bottom of your feet, and pull up dark green, cleansing earth energy. Pull this up and cleanse out each chakra starting with the root chakra and ending with the spiritual chakra on top of your head.

3. Your chakras are now wide open and clean.

4. Notice any sensations, images and feelings as you move into each chakra.

5. If you feel an imbalance or negative feeling, rub your hands together until they are warm, and place your hand on the chakra that needs universal healing energy.

6. Dial down each chakra to the percentages noted below to establish energy protection for the day.

7. Feel your heart and personal power center expand out to set your aura. See how far from the outline of your body you feel is safe and appropriate for you for each day. This is also unique and individual.

Setting Chakras

There are many depictions of chakras that allow you to imagine the wheel spinning. It opens and closes from the center. When the chakras are wide open and clean, the whole center is open. As you dial down each chakra, the middle of the wheel closes.

Here is the format and how I learned to set chakras. You may have your own method. This is an intuitive process, so get in touch with the wisdom of your body, as this is a guideline only.

Root Chakra (1st) Red - This is the energy center for survival, health and well-being, and tribal health. Set to 15 percent so you keep your life force energy strong for you.

Sacral Chakra (2nd) Orange - Your energy center for creativity, sex and emotional balance. Set to 25 percent, open it wider when you are in a safe place to express yourself creatively, sexually and emotionally.

Solar Plexus Chakra (3rd) Yellow - This is related to your personal power and where you get information about your "gut feelings." Set to 35 percent and tune into your intuition.

Heart Chakra (4th) Green - Unconditional love and forgiveness is vital for your heart energy. Set to 45 percent with the affirmation "I am so filled with self-love and compassion that it spills over into love and compassion for others."

Throat Chakra (5th) Blue - This energy center relates to your self-expression and communication. Set it to 80 percent, and speak what needs to be spoken.

Third Eye Chakra (6th) Purple - The energy of this center helps to create clarity about your truth without the taught traditions, beliefs and customs. Set to 80 percent, and be brave enough to live in your own truth.

Crown Chakra (7th) Pink - This connects your energy with the divine energy of the universe. Set to 15 percent and let yourself trust that your highest self is connected to the Source (whatever you might call that).

Once we become aware of an energy system within us, we are able to channel certain energies to have a sensual experience in ordinary life. Most people have done this with eating. Have you ever had a meal you called orgasmic?

When I traveled to Europe to launch the "Living an Organic and Orgasmic Life" tour, I was researching some things prior to going and found a restaurant in Barcelona, Spain, with the tag line "Organic is Orgasmic." I had to go speak to Antonia Moreno of Antonia's Organic Restaurant because she was PULSING something special out into the world.

Antonia didn't speak any English, so her beautiful daughter, Shell, interpreted. Antonia learned to cook through her mother. She saw the way she prepared food so well, and learned to love food. She learned to cook organically 14 years ago, and at that time her methods were considered strange because she was always concerned about cooking naturally without chemicals. Raising her daughters, she also used herbs instead of medicine when they were sick.

Her tag line was created when her daughter's friends said this food is so good you should call it "organic is orgasmic." And so it was.

When asked what makes her life orgasmic, she said she is in love with her business, friends, food, daughters, everything that she has created. She said it is not only sleeping with someone that is orgasmic. She is quite a character, and cracked a big smile when she said that making love is like in and out and so short. Eating can be stretched out and enjoyed orgasmically from beginning to end. She elaborately described the concept of a food orgasm. When the food is good, you start chewing and salivating. You begin to think it's so good you want to swallow it immediately, but you hold off and savor it a little longer. That is considered a food orgasm to Antonia.

This, of course, is only one example of how you can channel your pleasure energy to an ordinary experience. What would it be like to become aware of your sensual energy and channel it into your work? Your children? Your pets? Driving on the freeway?

In Chapter 5, I have real-life examples of how women have channeled their beauty, sensuality and sexuality, and PULSED it out for their own orgasmic nature. You will also see how everyone around them gets to benefit.

Rx from Chapter 4

1) What do you see when you have wellness? What do you feel?
2) Experiment with having a food orgasm, Antonia style.

Chapter 5

Ground in the Truth

At this point, I do want to say that I am fully aware that women who have exterior beauty due to their genes do get more attention from potential romantic partners. We are programmed to consider certain characteristics beautiful and enjoy the visual experience of something beautiful. AND, we still get to decide what is beautiful, sensual and sexual to our eyes. There is beauty in all things, and some of us are more skilled at finding it. More important to remember is beauty's availability to everyone.

This chapter is all about grounding in the truth. By now, I trust you have uncovered a few areas of your life in which you see your beauty, sensuality and sexuality. If not, you need to immediately call me.

I really do understand that this process is not necessarily easy, as we have been trained so well to NOT see our beauty, sensuality and sexuality. That is why this chapter is titled "Ground in the Truth," and not "your truth." We see what we are trained to see, and often that is not the truth. We believe what we tell ourselves. Give yourself the gift of affirming your own unique beauty, sensuality and sexuality.

Let me tell you about a couple of powerful women who did affirm this, how it manifested in their own lives and how they PULSED their own special brand of magnificence into the world.

Kimberly Cain, author of the novel *Heaven*, is also a speaker, intuitive spiritual guide and professional singer. *Heaven* is a fascinating novel of an erotic dancer who has a deep connection to her inner spiritual life. Kimberly's programs focus on how we can move our sexy spirit and create the freedom to express it.

Kimberly agrees with the shift in how we see vulnerability and love. She said we are seeing a fall of dictatorship, fall of those who want to keep others under their thumb. The internet allows those world-wide, powerful connections. People are standing up all over with a new desire to be free.

When I probed about what she means by vulnerability, she said vulnerability is where we get our egos out of the way and channel our ability to allow our love to flow and create goodness. Ego chatter is always concerned with how others think of us, and the barriers go up for our vulnerability. Vulnerability allows us to connect. This is my ultimate vision of PULSING goodness into the world.

Kimberly made another important point about our internet world and our need for connection. In *Heaven* she writes, "As our information age intensifies, the greater our need for nakedness and wild abandonment." While we have this amazing ability to connect through the computer, it's all about balance. We still need to look into faces. The eyes are the window to the soul, and that is what we want to connect with. We cannot PULSE anything into the world when we are looking into our cell phone. We must remember to engage with the person we are sitting right across from.

A CD included with the novel featured a compilation of music from Kimberly's band. The music created the feeling of the novel, with music that helps you find an erotic dancer within. Don't worry, it is normal to fantasize in these ways. You don't have to become an erotic dancer to be moved by the idea of it. Music moves the body and creates the vibration to PULSE.

Here is how Kimberly explained it. Music is a symphony of movements, and movements are created to move the sensations and feelings from one place to another. Music can shift a feeling of melancholy to elation or vice versa, and it taps into our deepest emotions. Sexuality does the same thing. As we move our powerful bodies, we allow ourselves to be so conscious and non-judgmental. Encourage fantasy without judgment, and allow yourself to move with the flow of it. It's amazing what can emerge. They are like a river of sensation or buzz.

When we feel a buzz, we feel power, and it stirs up the energy. We are all dealing with past labels of what people have thought of us. Her powerful book has been one of Kimberly's unique contributions, and when you hear the interview, you will feel the buzz that she ignited for herself and PULSED out there to others through her music, dance, programs and book.

Women and music are a strong combination to PULSE good vibrations of pleasure for themselves and those around them. And, it gets us in our bodies.

The soulful voice of vocalist, songwriter, and producer N'Dea Davenport first emerged in 1991 when she became the front woman for the acid jazz British funk band, The Brand New Heavies.

Long before worldwide notoriety was present, she fell in love with music, dance, performing, and the arts. "I think I got involved in almost everything creatively I could do when I was in school to keep my mind busy and stay out of trouble. From sports to theater, you name it. I probably did it." A regular routine of piano and dance studies were the core of her development. Ironic as it is, singing would later be the focus of her affections.

As soon as it was possible to "break out," as she calls it, she left her hometown of Atlanta with little more than $300 en route to Los Angeles, with the primary goal of just going somewhere she had never been to alone. Little did she know that early sense of adventure would begin a chain of events that would change her life forever.

"I have really fantastic parents that exposed me to a lot of things growing up. Education and travel were important things in our household and travel was considered an extension of our education." With that background, she had the need to go and explore to see where she stacked up with the world.

She went to L.A., a place she never had been, and was received warmly for her talents. She said it was a great transition to learn the music business. She was young, fearless and intuitive. Her successes kept coming as she keenly watched how the music business worked, demonstrating her basic instincts of showing up on time with the confidence that she could do it. She referred to it as painting by numbers.

"Everyone living their dreams has tons of courage and overcomes any fears that might present themselves," she claimed.

In the course of trying to find her way, N'Dea was given lots of opportunities in dance, music and fashion in the subculture of L.A. These were times where she opened up to meet and connect with different people from different backgrounds. This led her to the club culture and signing with a recording label.

Another group signed with the label was the Brand New Heavies, and they were looking for a vocalist. She volunteered to sing and be featured on some of their music, and ended up in a long-term collaboration as the lead singer of the band. She moved to London, maintained a home base in the U.S., and began traveling all around the world.

Being in front of so many people and seeing the ways of cultures all over the world, N'Dea became an unofficial psychologist of people just by paying attention to how societies do things. She emphasized she was no authority, she only possessed strong intuitive senses that humans should really start to live in the moment and embrace what it going on in the bigger picture.

A final gem from my N'Dea interview was the idea of needing to stay continuously awake and aware, and be welcoming to people to share our good vibes with. PULSE, Baby, PULSE!

Here is a final word about an American symbol of beauty, sexuality and sensuality who did such a marvelous job PULSING her truth and affecting all those surrounding her.

Elizabeth Taylor, with her many accomplishments, was an icon for beauty and sexuality. She represents an amazing example of how powerful the combination of beauty and sexuality can be for a woman. Her classic films and TV appearances brought the essence of beauty and sexuality to our screens.

Her personal life, although wrought with unsuccessful marriages, also showed how powerfully men respond to women comfortable with their beauty and sexuality. Eight marriages show she got what she wanted, choosing each one of her mates. On a grander scale, the work she pioneered with HIV/AIDS is a clear example of a woman's ability to PULSE her womanness for good in the world.

And as a finishing touch on this chapter about the truth of you and your magnificence, I leave you with this poem.

Love After Love

> The time will come
> when, with elation,
> you will greet yourself arriving
> at your own door, in your own mirror,
> and each will smile at the other's welcome,
> and say, sit here. Eat.
>
> You will love again the stranger who was yourself.
> Give wine. Give bread. Give back your heart
> to itself, to the stranger who has loved you

all your life, whom you ignored
for another, who knows you by heart.
Take down the love letters from the bookshelf,

the photographs, the desperate notes,
Peel your own image from the mirror.
Sit. Feast on your life.

Derek Walcott Collected Poems 1948-1984

Now let's get crystal clear on how our energy is always PULSED at some level into the world, and how we can become conscious of its impact and influence.

Rx from Chapter 5

1) Put on a song that makes you move into your hips. What kind of energy would that be to PULSE into your daily activities?

2) Write out the poem at the end of this chapter and put it in a prominent place in your home, car, office. Read it daily for the next two weeks.

Chapter 6

How Your Energy Impacts and Influences Others

Your energy is always having an impact and influence, whether you are aware of it or not. Becoming aware of how your energy impacts others is a tremendous asset in all of your relationships and allows you to PULSE into the world with confidence and ease.

"If you think you are too small to have an impact, try going to bed with a mosquito."

- Anita Roddick

Dame Anita Roddick, DBE (23 October, 1942–10 September, 2007) was a British businesswoman, human rights activist and environmental campaigner best known as the founder of The Body Shop, a cosmetics company producing and retailing beauty products that helped shape ethical consumerism. The company was one of the first to prohibit the use of ingredients tested on animals and one of the first to promote fair trade with third world countries.

I guess Dame Anita knew a little bit about how to make an impact.

There are people I used to have in my closest circle who were very negative and had a prominent attitude of half-empty. As you can tell by now, I am an extremely optimistic person. It was the co-dependent people pleaser in me who felt it was my responsibility to balance out this negativity. I also had thoughts of helping turn around their negative attitudes. I was not effective AT ALL in either one of these endeavors. Instead of me raising the vibration of those around me, I ended up losing my own vibration, leaving me drained and exhausted.

"You can never really live anyone else's life, not even your child's. The influence you exert is through your own life, and what you've become yourself."

- *Eleanor Roosevelt*

Mrs. Roosevelt was certainly one wise woman.

What I notice when people are in a negative energy place is it can affect an entire room, even if they are not saying anything negative. When I was married, my husband never wanted to spend time with his family. As a result, he was sometimes, though not always, in a bad mood when we would get together with them. He would sit in the corner, put his head in a book so no one talked to him, and grumpily wait out the hours until it was time to leave.

His nonverbal energy was so strong that the entire room turned heavy. He thought no one noticed him and that if people would just leave him alone, all would be fine. That was not the case. His mood affected everyone, in part because there were times he could be so much fun and very lively during these events.

The same was true for our home life. He would often, again not always, be very put upon by houseguests. If he was in a good mood and liked the friends, he was like a stand-up comedian and everyone loved him. And when the opposite was true the emotions of everyone involved were so heavy, you could cut through the air with a knife.

I don't mean to pick on my ex-husband, really I don't, but he is just such a great example of nonverbal energy having either a positive or negative impact on the space. Everything you do has impact. Not a single movement or word goes unnoticed.

You don't want to hold yourself back from PULSING out there. I have spent all these words preparing you to be big. In my leadership program, we used to say, "Give yourself full permission and be responsible for your impact." And I would add, "Give yourself full permission to be into your beauty, sensuality and sexuality." It requires deep listening skills and a sensitivity to energy that is too much to cover in this book, but let me just give you the basics.

Your body is always speaking to you and others. Your body geography determines, in part, how you feel. Try this: sit in a chair, bend over, look at the floor, and talk about your dreams and big visions. How does it feel? For another experience, drop your arms to your side, open your chest, and look up at the sky, and talk about your dreams and big visions. Does that feel differently?

When you meet someone who smiles, extends a hand, looks you in the eye and says "hi," how does that feel? Consider another experience in meeting someone who has their arms crossed and looks down while saying "hi." Does this produce a different kind of impact?

Consider the impact you want to have on people.

When you want to influence and have people listen to you, an open stance with arms relaxed at your side, easy smile, and calm but clear voice is a great advantage. Can you feel how tuning into your beauty, sensuality and sexuality helps you do that? Our ability to influence is so much greater if we are walking our talk. You can't fake this. It has to be authentic.

This is especially true when it comes to our children. Your kids, especially after age 10, are no longer really listening to you. They are watching you. That's why I love these two verses from the Dixie Chicks' song "I Hope."

> 'Cause our children are watching us
> They put their trust in us
> They're gonna be like us
> So let's learn from our history
> And do it differently
>
> Our children are watching us
> They put their trust in us
> They're gonna be like us
> Its okay for us to disagree
> We can work it out lovingly'

The very best energy of all to model is the energy of gratitude.

According to Wikipedia, "the systematic study of gratitude within psychology only began around the year 2000, possibly because psychology has traditionally been focused more on understanding distress rather than understanding positive emotions." Given that, it makes sense that we are still learning about how to feel grateful.

In my experience, it is definitely a practice. There are times when gratitude comes easy for me, and there are times when it can be hard to muster.

It is worth the effort though, as empirical findings show that grateful people are more likely to have higher levels of happiness and lower levels of stress and depression.

Statistics from World Poverty report that, "if you have a full fridge, clothes on your back, a roof over your head and a place to sleep, you are wealthier than 75 percent of the world's population."

Gratitude is a perspective, and so it is a choice to feel grateful. When you review the evidence above, it seems like it should be second nature to feel grateful.

And, even with all this evidence, there are times in my life where it can be difficult to choose gratitude. For example, when I have worked diligently on a project and the result is less than what I wanted, I often choose disappointment. And then I collect all sorts of evidence to support my disappointment. This, too, is my choice.

How do I shift from disappointment to gratitude?

1. PAUSE and feel where the tension is in my body, because disappointment always equals tension in my body.

2. Acknowledge the tension and breathe into it with the intention of releasing and relaxing.

3. Remind myself that life is a series of experiences and it is ALWAYS my choice how to respond and learn from them.

4. Become present with the moment. Note the food in the fridge, the clothes on my back, the home I am living in, and the bed I get to sleep in.

5. Smile at my humanness and embrace the wild journey of life … living an organic and orgasmic life, that is.

May you find the gratitude in simple things today, like being able to take another breath and experience another amazing day on this planet!

The grand finale chapter of this series of books will focus on how each one of us can contribute to the global healing that is underway on the planet.

Rx from Chapter 6

1) Stand in front of the mirror and practice an open stance with arms relaxed at your side, easy smile, and calm but clear voice. Then approach someone who you would like to influence in some way (take you out to dinner, discuss something meaningful to you, etc.) and notice the results. I would love to hear your experience.

2) The next time you find yourself complaining or whining, try the five steps from disappointment to gratitude.

   1. PAUSE and feel where the tension is in your body, because disappointment always equals tension in the body.

   2. Acknowledge the tension and breathe into it with the intention of releasing and relaxing.

   3. Remind yourself that life is a series of experiences and it is ALWAYS your choice how to respond and learn from them.

   4. Become present with the moment. Note the food in the fridge, the clothes on your back, the home you are living in, and the bed you get to sleep in.

   5. Smile at your humanness and embrace the wild journey of life … living an organic and orgasmic life, that is.

Putting It All Together

Moving to A Global Healing

I write this final piece on the final day of 2013. My New Year's resolution is to commit to doing everything I can to contribute to a global healing. There are many things happening all over the world that are moving us toward healing. Look for them.

Simply put, the picture I want to paint for a global healing is to see women and men feeling peaceful, passionate and fully conscious of their inner pleasure. Making it a priority to PAUSE and ground this feeling every day, then PONDER the gratitude of feeling beautiful, sensual and sexual every day. From there, your magnificence will easily PULSE from your bright light out into the world.

I am on a mission to eradicate our attachment to pain and open us up to more pleasure and positivity. I don't believe we can tackle the problems and issues that confront our lives and our world today from a place of fear and negativity. That's how we got here to being with, right?

Global healing also requires men and women to have a greater understanding of each other. Have you ever experienced an encounter with the opposite sex where you felt like you were communicating so precisely, in direct language, and your intentions were completely misconstrued? Okay, it is a rhetorical question. How can we learn to understand and honor our differences with love, compassion and an open heart? My intention is to keep the conversation moving in a healthy way.

Masculine and feminine characteristics are clearly very different energies. A man who exudes strong masculinity is often a lone wolf, independent, competitive, physically strong, forgetful, logical, tough, and acutely self-aware. What I mean by acutely self-aware is a focus on taking care of his needs without consideration of what his female companion might need. Some call this self-centered, but I don't, as it is also negative to ignore the many good things about taking care of your own needs.

What you will notice with women who live from an extreme feminine place is a gentle collaborator, nurturing, loving, adapting and empathizing with a relaxed receptivity to change. Often women are co-dependent because they receive what comes to them with the intention of nurturing and loving it back into balance. It's a woman's intuition that allows her to feel what is out of balance. The generous way a woman serves in this capacity is a beautiful thing. However, if a woman is not tuned into her own needs and inner nature or intuition, life can easily become unhealthy in relationship with a man.

This is far from an exhaustive list of characteristics, and yet the stark contrast of energies is apparent. We all carry both energies within, and each person has a unique spot on the spectrum from extreme masculine to extreme feminine. From the extremes noted here, it is no wonder women lose their identity in relationships and men are so confused by women and their flip-flop behavior.

For global healing to happen, we need to step up to our individual responsibility and honor one another.

What is the role of women?

BE thankful for your body! You have this one and only body to live in as the person you are today. Take care of it, nurture it, and love yourself up from head to toe. Treat your body like a sacred temple.

Rediscovering your inner beauty, sensuality and sexuality is essential for global healing to take place. If women are not comfortable with themselves, stressed out and feeling dried up, then that is how the earth will feel, too. Mother earth relies on feminine energy to stay nourished.

The main areas that fall between you and your inner beauty, sensuality and sexuality are:

    1 - The media

    2 - Your own negative thinking

    3 - The story you tell yourself

When we get clear about the unreal images in the media, when we make an active effort in our minds to experience pleasure and write a new, more authentic story for ourselves, then we are well on our way to creating a new world. We have learned from the laws of attraction and conscious research that our thoughts, feelings and actions create the world as we know it. What kind of world do you want to live in?

The role of the woman is to PULSE your beauty, sensuality and sexuality while honoring men. During the live show of "Living an Organic and Orgasmic Life," I asked all the women to stand and look at the men around them, and repeat after me: "I respect your magnificent masculinity. Without you, I would not be here. My understanding of our differences helps me to appreciate your sexual energy."

What is the role of the man?

As I understand men and their energies, I see a strength in mind and body that is calming and peaceful to my inner soul. There is a determination that I admire from the toughness and competitive male stance. Forgetfulness is a vulnerable and innocent place that has a sweet honesty. These are the perceptions and attitudes I am embracing to fully appreciate and love our amazing men.

During the same live show both in Europe and the U.S., I asked all the men to stand and take in the beauty of women around them and repeat after me: "I honor you as a woman and embrace your feminine nature. I want to support your happiness. I would like to create a positive and constructive relationship with you."

We need to take responsibility individually for the impact of our own true nature and rebalance ourselves. The world needs our best efforts. I am curious how our communication would change with the ability to stand in each other's shoes and see the positive side of our opposing characteristics.

What is the role of the children?

How can we encourage our children to look within to their beautiful souls for how they feel instead of their appearance? I had the amazing opportunity to coach a woman on air about her inner beauty. She was the mother of three girls, and I emphasized the importance of her feeling her beauty. It wasn't enough to just talk about being beautiful with her girls, she needed to live it.

Here is the blog post she wrote about her coaching homework:

Staring in the Mirror, Yet I Couldn't See
by Tia Silverthorn Bach
DepressionCookies.com

It seemed a simple instruction—look in the mirror and say, "You are a self-confident, graceful, creative and inspiring person." Coach Betty laid out the guidelines for finding inner beauty. I was pumped. How hard could it be?

I steadied myself in front of the mirror, armed with the words and the will. "You are…" What is that, I thought, a new wrinkle? Crap, there's another gray hair. I pulled at my skin for a few minutes. I looked tired, sad even. My eyes scanned down. More pounds, I wondered and swore my t-shirt fit better a month ago.

"Mom, whatcha doing," my sweet six-year-old asked, confused as to why I was pulling, squirming and grimacing.

What was I doing? I was supposed to be lifting myself up, and all I could focus on were my flaws. If one of my three beautiful daughters did that, I would point out every wonderful attribute, every blessing. Yet, I focused on all the things I tell my children not to . . . physical attributes, not inner beauty.

My mother and I co-wrote a coming of age novel, "Depression Cookies," showcasing two distinct points of view: teenage daughter and her mother. I wrote the teenage daughter's point of view while my mom wrote the mother's. Our hope was to open up the dialogue not only between mothers and daughters, but all women to discuss what makes us special and unique, what binds us.

Plus, I'm raising three daughters. It's easy to tell them to love themselves, but we parents know kids do what they see, not what they are told. Same is true for writers, we are constantly told to show and not tell. It means nothing to tell my children, and other women, to love themselves if I can't show them how I love myself.

"[Kids] don't remember what you try to teach them. They remember what you are."
  - Jim Henson

I believe whole-heartedly in inner beauty, but I need to practice what I preach . . . for myself, for my three children, for my friends and family.

I started to soften in the mirror, gave my daughter a hug, and repeated, "You ARE a self-confident, graceful, creative and inspiring person."

"Me, too, Mama," my sweet daughter repeated. We were both standing in front of the mirror, and I finally started to see. I decided to give my children their own sayings so we could practice together. We're committed to this exercise every day until our images become clearer and the words easier to say. It's a beginning, but a good one.

How do you allow yourself to make the journey to inner beauty, sensuality, and sexuality, fear and all? How do you stay focused on the greater vision that's more important than the fear?

The questions go together. Being brave and doing uncomfortable things relies on the fact that there is a goal greater than your fears.

The way of PAUSE, PONDER & PULSE is a certain journey to Global Healing, and on the path, you will undoubtedly increase your pleasure.

Resources

Websites

http://www.CoachBettyLive.com/

http://onetaste.us/

MadlyinLovewithme.com

BernieSiegel.com

PlanetSARK.com or call her inspiration line at 415-546-3742

Kim "Skipper" Corbin at http://www.iskip.com

DebraReble.com

SoulHeartedPartnership.com

SandraHickman.com

FreddieRavel.com

YossiFine.com

Ti Harmon at tiharmonmusic.com & Facebook.com/tiharmonmusic

www.TheSensualLife.com

Sign up for Monica Day's free report and weekly e-zine to start tapping into your own sensuality right away. It is easier than you think!

www.titilayoadedokun.com

www.matstein.com

www.kimberlycain.com

www.marianne.com

www.thebiggergame.com

Meditations

Relax meditations – http://tinyurl.com/mt3enoh

http://www.amazon.com/Relax-Guided-Meditations-Stress-Anxiety/dp/B001JTU4RA/ref=sr_1_3?ie=UTF8&qid=1381864431&sr=8-3&keywords=bonnie+groessl

RELAX digital remedy - www.sandrahickman.com

Information on Breathwork

http://www.goodtherapy.org/breathwork.html

Books

"Wherever You Go, There You Are," by Jon Kabat Zinn

"Don't Just Do Something, Sit There," by Sylvia Boorstein

"You Can Heal Your Life," by Louise Hay

"The Power of Now," by Eckhart Tolle

"Red Hot and Holy," by Sera Beak

"Return to Love," by Marianne Williamson

"Heaven," by Kimberly Cain

YouTube Videos

"My Stroke of Insight," Jill Bolte Taylor

http://www.youtube.com/watch?v=mYD7Y9CXeUw

Neuroanatomist Jill Bolte Taylor had an opportunity few brain scientists would wish for: One morning, she realized she was having a massive stroke. As it happened – as she felt her brain functions slip away one by one, speech, movement, understanding – she studied and remembered every moment. This is a powerful story about how our brains define us and connect us to the world and to one another.

"Orgasm: The Cure for Hunger in the Western Woman," Nicole Daedone

http://www.youtube.com/watch?v=s9QVq0EM6g4

Nicole Daedone is a sought-after speaker, author, and educator focusing on the intersection between orgasm, intimacy, and life. She is the founder of OneTaste, a cutting-edge company bringing a new definition of orgasm to women. The practice at the heart of her work is called OM or Orgasmic Meditation. OM uniquely combines the tradition of extended orgasm with Nicole's own interest in Zen Buddhism, mystical Judaism and semantics. Helping to foster a new conversation about orgasm — one that's real, relevant, and intelligent — she has inspired thousands of students to make OM a part of their everyday lives.

"The Power of Vulnerable," Brene Brown

http://www.youtube.com/watch?v=iCvmsMzlF7o

Brene Brown studies human connection – our ability to empathize, belong, love. In a poignant, funny talk at TEDxHouston, she shares a deep insight from her research, one that sent her on a personal quest to know herself as well as to understand humanity. A talk to share.

"Looks Aren't Everything. Believe Me, I'm a Model," Cameron Russell
http://www.youtube.com/watch?v=KM4Xe6DlpOY

Cameron Russell admits she won "a genetic lottery." She's tall, pretty and an underwear model. But don't judge her by her looks. In this fearless talk, she takes a wry look at the industry that had her looking highly seductive at barely 16 years old. (Filmed at TEDxMidAtlantic.)

PAUSING for Pleasure, Betty Louise

Video 1: http://www.youtube.com/watch?v=N8U-hYx0_Ik

Video2: http://www.youtube.com/watch?v=Bm8lZQy9zls

Video3: http://www.youtube.com/watch?v=yS3sxmfqixY

Tiny url http://tinyurl.com/lz7vlek

Deepest Fear Quote, Betty Louise

http://www.youtube.com/watch?v=hrtJtty2LsU

Movie trailer for MissRepresentation
http://www.youtube.com/watch?v=S5pM1fW6hNs

Movie trailer for Orgasmic, Inc.
http://orgasminc.org/about-synopsis.php?trailer=true

Kimberly Cain/REALM Gathering
http://youtu.be/IU5PFBdEYwg

Links to complete interviews can be found at www.CoachBettyLive.com

About the Author

Coach Betty Louise, Wellness Coach and U.S. radio personality, has coached and interviewed progressive thinking experts, artists and innovators from all over the world. Author John Gray of Mars/Venus fame, Grammy Award-winning artist Freddie Ravel, and brain researchers Jill Bolte Taylor and Dr. Louann Brizendine have been some of her amazing guests.

She earned her credentials at the Coaches Training Institute (CTI), the CTI Co-Active Leadership Program, the Center for Right Relationship (CRR), and the Academy of Intuition Medicine. She is also a Master Trainer for the Stanford Chronic Disease Self-Management Program and co-author of the book "Understanding Fibromyalgia: A Guide for Family and Friends."

Betty is an ecologically minded coach who works with women and mindful men to rediscover their inner beauty, sensuality, and sexuality so that they fall in love with themselves every time they look in the mirror. Her phone and Skype sessions and teleseminars open you up to the possibility of living an organic and orgasmic life with courage, confidence and grace.

She spends her time in Phoenix, San Francisco Bay Area, and Seattle, where she lives organically and orgasmically with friends and family. She has an amazing grown daughter who is a guiding light in her life. To stay in touch with Coach Betty Louise, you can sign up for her email list on her website, www.CoachBettyLive.com.

www.ingramcontent.com/pod-product-compliance
Lightning Source LLC
Chambersburg PA
CBHW071621080526
44588CB00010B/1220